A VISIT

TO

JAPAN, CHINA, AND INDIA

A VISIT

TO

JAPAN, CHINA, AND INDIA.

ROBERT NICHOLAS FOWLER, M.A., F.R.G.S., F.S.A.

GYAN

Published by

Gyan Publishing House
5, Ansari Road
Daryaganj, New Delhi-110002
Phone: 011-47034999, 9811692060
E-mail: books@gyanbooks.com

Distribution Network
gyanbooks.com
India, USA, Canada, UK, Australia, France

ISBN : 978-81-212-9759-2 (PB)
First Published, 1877

2nd Impression 2023

Printed at: Gyan Press, Delhi.

A VISIT TO JAPAN , CHINA, AND INDIA
Author: ROBERT NICHOLAS FOWLER

A VISIT

TO

JAPAN, CHINA, AND INDIA.

A VISIT

TO

JAPAN, CHINA, AND INDIA.

BY

ROBERT NICHOLAS FOWLER, M.A., F.R.G.S., F.S.A.

FELLOW OF UNIVERSITY COLLEGE, LONDON.

1877.

PREFACE.

So many travellers round the world have published their journals, that an apology is required for adding to the list. My excuse must be that I have taken the opportunity to allude to a number of questions of public interest in which, both in and out of Parliament, I have for many years taken a deep interest.

Gastard, Chippenham,
November, 1876.

CONTENTS.

A VISIT TO JAPAN, CHINA, AND INDIA.

CHAPTER I.

FROM LONDON TO JAPAN.

I LEFT London on Wednesday, the 1st of September, 1875, and at one o'clock on Thursday, the 2nd, sailed from Liverpool in the Inman steamer "City of Chester," Captain Leitch. The day was wet and misty, and the night very dark, so that Captain Leitch, being unable to see the Tuscar, very wisely kept in mid-channel, though it took him out of his course. The next day was beautifully fine, as we entered Queenstown Harbour, where we saw the remains of the fleet anchored, and heard of that unfortunate collision in a fog similar to that we had passed through, which occasioned the loss of the "Vanguard." We were detained at Queenstown for several hours, waiting for the arrival of the mail, which gave us the opportunity of driving round the neighbourhood, and visiting Cork. The mail came on board in the afternoon, so we sailed about five, and at nine passed the Fastnets light, and took leave of the coast of Ireland.

It was my first voyage across the Atlantic, and in a company of more than 200 cabin passengers I hardly met any one who had not made the passage before. I apprehend, however, that our voyage was an ordinary specimen of the sail across the Atlantic. The weather was generally fine, and the passengers amused themselves as well as they could, though the large number on board occasioned some inconveniences. The "City of Chester" is a very fine boat of 4600 tons. Her best day's run was 346 miles, her worst 317. The day's run gives rise to a good deal of betting, which I was afterwards told was not always fair. The passengers were mostly Americans, and I heard long and earnest discussions on the state of politics, and the chances of the next Presidential election. On Sunday Captain Leitch, who is a fine seaman and a courteous gentleman, read the Church service in the cabin. This service in the midst of the ocean was solemn and striking. About five o'clock in the afternoon of the 10th, a pilot-boat appeared. It was a beautiful sight to see the fine cutter manœuvre, and the pilot put off in a little cockleshell of a boat which rode like a cork on the long waves. It shows the pluck of the New York pilots to come out nearly 600 miles to meet ships. At daylight on Sunday, the 12th, we saw the American land before us, and reached Sandy Hook light-house after a passage from Queenstown of eight days, eighteen hours. The sail up the bay to New York is lovely, as the shores are beautiful, and the city magnificent. About half-past eight we reached New York, when I took leave of my fellow-passengers, with whom I had passed a pleasant week, and landed on American ground. The United States custom-house is not the common-place affair it is in most countries. The duties on many articles are enormous, and Americans returning from Europe have often made extensive purchases. Luckily for me, I had very little luggage, so I passed the ordeal without difficulty, and reached the Fifth Avenue Hotel just in time to attend church. It was pleasant in a foreign land to be using the glorious liturgy we are accustomed to at home, and to be able to thank God that He had so far sped me on my way.

Next day I made an excursion to Burlington, New Jersey, to visit a relative, whom I was not so fortunate as to find at home. Crossing the Hudson in pouring rain, by one of the gigantic steam ferries, which are a feature of New York, I took "the cars" (to use the expressive American phrase) at Jersey City, and proceeded through a fine park-like country, interspersed with pretty towns, to Trenton, where we left the Philadelphia line, and followed the beautiful banks of the Delaware to Burlington, a foreign-looking town, where the houses reminded me of Holland, but the vegetation was that of a southern clime.

I remained in New York till the morning of Wednesday, the 15th, and greatly admired that city of palaces. Broadway, which extends for upwards of four miles, is a magnificent street, with splendid buildings, and the Central Park is very large, and in parts beautiful. The tramways which traverse the streets are very convenient; but it is remarkable that New York, in common, I believe, with other American cities, is deficient in good street conveyances. In Europe we are accustomed to be carried cheap; but here, the only carriages plying for hire are lumbering chariots, worthy of the days of Louis XIV., which charge rates that are altogether prohibitory. In fact, everything here gives evidence of a country where money is easily made and carelessly spent. The hotels are magnificent, but their charges are enormous, and the system of making you pay so much per diem, without reference to whether you take your meals or not, is very objectionable.

I was anxious to leave San Francisco by the steamer of October 1st, and I therefore had only eighteen days to spend in America. I concluded it would be better to devote what time I had to the Pacific States, and to leave the Eastern for a future journey. Two lines of railway lead from New York to Niagara—the Erie, of which we have lately heard so much in the City, and the New York Central. I selected the latter because it follows the beautiful scenery of the Hudson, which the Americans are fond of comparing to the Rhine. I do not think the comparison very appropriate, as it is a much broader river, and seemed to me more to resemble the Lake of Neuchatel. Winding along the lovely banks, we reached the fine city of Albany, where we left the river, and, traversing a country which, by its wooded aspect, showed that it had been formerly a forest, and passing towns boasting the classic names of Rome, Utica, and Syracuse, arrived at Niagara. The American railways are very comfortable, though they have nominally only one class. The Pulman cars, however, are attached to each train, in which you can travel at an extra fare. These cars, which have lately been introduced on the Midland, give you comfortable sofas or armchairs by day, and sleeping-berths by night. The American fares are, I believe, low in the Eastern States; but on the line from Omaha to San Francisco the charge is 100 dollars, which, though it is at a higher rate than we are accustomed to in Europe, is not unreasonable, considering the difficulties under which it has been constructed. The system which enables you to take a ticket at New York for San Francisco, with liberty to stop at any station you please, is a great convenience.

After sleeping at the Niagara Hotel on the American side, I started to visit the Falls. I should recommend any one with leisure to establish himself for two or three days at the Clifton Hotel on the Canada side, where the cataract can be seen to the greatest advantage. The transit from one side to the other is accomplished by a suspension bridge. The American Fall is exceedingly beautiful, while the Horse Shoe on the Canada side is, I suppose, unquestionably the finest in the world, unless that of the Zambesi, discovered by Dr. Livingstone, must be excepted, though the great volume of spray rising from it is a hindrance to its being appreciated. After walking under the Fall, and admiring the magnificent view from the top of a house close to the Horse Shoe, we drove to the Rapids, about two miles below the Falls, and then to the Whirlpool. The latter is an extraordinary sight, as the river, after running straight from the Falls for some three miles, apparently comes to an end; but on proceeding a little further you perceive that it turns at right angles very suddenly, and that the turn occasions a whirlpool. I was familiar with the Horse Shoe from pictures; but this sudden bend, of which I did not recollect to have heard, surprised and delighted me. Niagara is among the greatest wonders of this beautiful world, though the surrounding country is not remarkable for scenery. Still, when I remember Moore's enraptured description,—

> "These are miracles which man,
> Caged in the bounds of Europe's pigmy plan,
> Can scarcely dream of, which his eye must see
> To know how beautiful this world can be,"—

I think he never can have gazed on those sublime Alpine scenes with which, in these days, every English tourist is familiar.

While we were at the Rapids it began to rain, and when the train left the Suspension Bridge station it had increased to such a storm as I have rarely witnessed. The railway is carried over the river by a suspension bridge—a triumph of engineering skill. The Great Western Railway of Canada carried us past the end of Lake Ontario, through a country of forests, where the stations bear the English names of Grimsby, Woodstock, London, and Chatham, to Windsor, when the train was ferried over by a steam bridge to Detroit. I deeply regretted that time did not permit me to remain in Canada, because I feel that everything which concerns that great dominion should be of interest to an Englishman. Our great object should be to draw closer those ties which unite Canada to our common sovereign and our common country.

The journey from Virginia to Salt Lake City occupied between four and five days of continuous travelling. After leaving Detroit, passing through the States of Michigan and Indiana, we reached Chicago, where Lake Michigan was breaking on the shore like a stormy sea. Owing to the train being an hour and a half late, I lost the opportunity of driving through this wonderful city, which in three years has been rebuilt after the great fire. I believe its great sight is what was at that moment the largest hotel in the world, though it has subsequently been eclipsed by one at San Francisco. We proceeded across the State of Illinois, through a fine agricultural country, though dull, flat, and destitute of trees, and about nightfall crossed the magnificent stream of the Mississippi to the town of Burlington, in Iowa. Next morning we reached Council Bluffs, on the eastern side of the Missouri, and crossing that river by a very long bridge, rendered necessary by the sand-banks through which its shifting current winds, reached Omaha. The tide of American settlers is constantly sweeping West, so that what a few years ago was a back-wood station is now a flourishing city; but at the present time Omaha may fairly be considered as the spot where civilization terminates, and you enter on the dismal prairies. Three railways from Chicago converge at Council Bluffs, while the Union Pacific is the only line beyond Omaha.

We continued our journey across the prairies, where is much fine land, which some day will be productive; but these long, rolling, monotonous tracts, without a tree to be seen, are very uninteresting. Where there are some inhabitants, herds of cattle graze, and antelopes and prairie dogs are to be seen; but the Indian and the buffalo, who formerly tenanted these wilds, have disappeared. Much as this railway does for present convenience, it is sad to think it is at the expense of the ancient and lawful owners of the country. Nor are they replaced by better men, as the new-comers are often among the most lawless of mankind. We had three prisoners in the train, who had been arrested for committing a murder, and who narrowly escaped being lynched. Along this route in former days the Mormons and other emigrants toiled in waggons, displaying the virtue of indomitable perseverance. The scene is dreary as the Russian steppes between Moscow and Odessa; but what is very remarkable is, that the line attains the great elevation of 8250 feet above the level of the sea by a gradual ascent, without terraces or other engineering works. After crossing the last chain of the Rocky Mountains, we left the prairies and descended through charming ravines, which reminded me of the Valley of the Tchernaya in the Crimea, to the junction station of Ogden. The absence of trees through the whole route is very remarkable. What is called the 1000-mile tree is situated some four or five miles from the 1000-mile post, and I presume is so called from the difficulty of finding one nearer. On the other hand, the rocks are magnificent, and one is occasionally carried through scenes of wild grandeur.

At Ogden the Union Pacific Railway from Omaha meets the Central Pacific Railway from San Francisco, while a short line takes you to Salt Lake City, the Mormon capital. My train was impeded, in traversing this line, by a tremendous storm of wind, but I arrived about 10 p.m. on Sept. 20, and took up my quarters at the Townsend House. In America, hotels frequently bear the name of the owner. The Walker House, the rival hotel, is in the hands of the Gentiles, between whom and the Mormons there seems great hostility.

At supper I had a long conversation with my landlord, who came with the early settlers from Nauvoo, and settled here twenty-three years ago, though since that time he has been on a mission to England. The hardships which these early settlers must have endured in passing through the wilderness which the railway now traverses prove them to have been influenced by strong fanaticism. He told me that the population of the city consisted of 25,000 Mormons and of 3000 Gentiles. He said they accept the Bible *in its liberal sense,* holding the Book of Mormon to be a supplementary revelation in regard to the Church in America. He defended polygamy as a check on immorality.

Next morning I ascended a hill overlooking the town, which presented a striking appearance. It is laid out in blocks of ten acres, with eight houses to each block, so that every house has one and a quarter acres of land. These are traversed by streets at right angles, through which water is carried, while tramways are laid down in the leading thoroughfares. The town lies like an oasis in a valley, with barren snow-capped mountains around it, and the Salt Lake in the distance. Whatever we may think of the Mormons, we must do justice to the energy which has converted a wilderness into a smiling garden. The Tabernacle is an immense building, capable of seating 13,000 people. It was hung round with texts of Scripture and moral sentences, while the roof was decorated with imitations of flowers. It would have been interesting to have been here on a Sunday, and to have heard a Mormon sermon. Near it the Temple, another religious edifice, is being slowly built.

I called on the Hon. James Cucannon, the representative of the territory of Utah in Congress, where he sits with the right of speaking, but not of voting. I found him a very superior and intelligent man, and was much interested in his views on American politics and the chances of the next Presidential election, as from his position he was able to take a more dispassionate view of the state of affairs than most of those whom I have met with. I had failed to get a letter of introduction to Brigham Young, or, as he is here designated, "His Excellency President Young," and therefore made no attempt to see that extraordinary personage, though I should have much liked to do so. The ride back to Ogden along the banks of the lake was striking from the clear, serene atmosphere, and the graceful shapes of the mountains.

From Ogden I proceeded towards San Francisco, a journey of forty-eight hours. The train stops for meals, which are dignified with the names of "breakfast," "dinner," and "supper," and are charged a dollar each. Every meal, however, is alike, consisting of beefsteaks, pancakes, and coffee. Our ride on the 22nd lay through plains which abound in alkali, and, the day being hot and dry, the dust was very unpleasant. The only vegetation seemed to be sage-grass. The absence of trees continued, and the only difficulty the engineers appear to have encountered has been to protect the line from snow, which requires fences and long galleries. On this day, for the first time, we saw Indians begging at the station. It was a most melancholy sight to behold the remnants of a once noble and powerful race sunk to the lowest state of degradation. We sometimes hear it said that it is a law of nature that the feebler races of mankind should be extinguished by advancing civilization. To me this appears a hollow and worthless excuse for the cupidity and rapacity of mankind. Civilization professes to aim at the elevation and improvement of the human race, while by the precepts of our holy religion we are commanded not to defraud or go beyond our neighbours in anything. Can it then be said that the only way to elevate the earth is to improve the weaker race of man off its face? Such a doctrine is a disgrace to civilization, a violation of the principles of Christianity. I know that the improvement of aboriginal tribes is an undertaking of great difficulty; but missionaries going forth in dependence on the help of God have been blessed in their arduous labours, while the State is bound to afford them justice and protection. In this duty most governments have lamentably failed. It is only justice to the Washington Government to say that they have been honourably distinguished by their anxiety to promote the welfare of the Indians, and President Grant in particular has striven to pursue a humane policy. In our own country, King William the Fourth ought to be gratefully remembered for his declaration to Lord Glenelg, in regard to the Caffres, that "he would not have his dominions extended by injustice;" while in France the policy of the unfortunate Emperor Napoleon the Third, in regard to the Arabs of Algeria, deserved the admiration of every friend of humanity. But while, in both the New and the Old World, individual rulers have endeavoured to promote the interests of those who have none to protect them, most States have allowed the aborigines to become the prey of the settlers. A quarrel springs up between a settler and a native. It is easy for a man of some education to put the poor native technically in the wrong. The State takes the part of the settler, and either by regular troops, or merely by the exertions of the emigrants, the natives are expelled from their country, or perhaps wholly exterminated. Such, alas! is the process which has gone on in whatever part of the world civilization has come in contact with barbarous men. Everywhere we see what Macaulay called "the most affecting of human spectacles—the strength of civilization without its mercy." The aborigines are conquered and enslaved, and drunkenness completes the destruction which oppression has begun.

Such has been the history of the destruction of the Indian tribes along the Pacific route. Here they were confronted with men possessing the energy of the American character, but also possessing that recklessness too often found in those who prefer the wild life of the back-woods to the monotony of a highly-civilized community. The Washington Government was distant, and, if it had the power, had not the will to interfere between its own citizens and the Indians. Consequently, after many hard contests, they have been deprived of their country, and whisky is completing the ruin of this once-powerful people. They are now thrust back on reservations which Congress has set aside for them, and where, it is to be hoped, effectual measures will be taken for their protection and improvement.

During the night we passed Reno, the junction for Virginia City, celebrated for those wonderful silver-mines whose productiveness is now disturbing the currency. I should have much liked to visit them, but unfortunately the time at my disposal did not permit it. On waking next morning, I found myself in a snow-shed, where the train was stopping, owing, as I afterwards learned, to another snow-shed having been on fire, and blocking up the way. In this part of the line it is continually necessary to carry it through long galleries as a protection against the winter snow. The descent of the Sierra Nevada into the plains of California is a triumph of engineering skill amid lovely views. We rounded a mountain called Cape Horn, down which the railway is carried to the town of Colfax. The scenery is certainly very grand, and to an American, particularly to an inhabitant of the vast plains of the Central States, it must appear stupendous, but to an Englishman who has traversed the railroads over the Simmering and the Brenna, over the Apennines and the Black Forest, and who has crossed the wonderful roads which span the Alps, while it recalls many familiar scenes of sublimity and beauty, it has not the charm of novelty.

At Colfax the train stopped for breakfast, and here I took the opportunity to convert my remaining greenbacks into gold. I found the question of hard money against inflation was exciting great interest; the commercial Eastern States as a rule advocating the former, the Western States the latter. I was told by a gentleman that the Western States wanted money for railways and other purposes, which they must raise in Europe, and therefore it was necessary in their interests to maintain greenbacks. I remarked that the Western States made a great mistake if they supposed that inflation, as the suspension of cash payments is called, would assist them to raise money. European capitalists like to know what interest they will receive, and they will grant much better terms if that interest is paid in gold than if it is left to a shifting, uncertain rate of currency. It seems extraordinary, in a rich country like the United States, to find every transaction, down to a few cents., carried on in paper, and no effort made to return to the system of cash payments, or, as they call it, hard money, which prevails in every other prosperous country. In the Pacific States, with their large supplies of the precious metals, they naturally repudiate greenbacks, though they have bank notes, like our own, convertible into gold. All payments are here made in gold instead of currency. They have gold coins for as large a sum as twenty dollars (4*l.*). It struck me that it might be worth the consideration of our own Chancellor of the Exchequer, whether pieces of five sovereigns might not be useful in England.

Leaving the beautiful scenery around Colfax, the hills became gradually lower till at last we reached a plain where the burnt-up aspect showed that we were in a southern clime. Passing the fine city of Sacramento, the State capital of California, I stopped at Lathrop, a junction station in the midst of a desolate plain, where I was detained several hours, with little to do but to contemplate a bear kept here for the amusement of the public. At length the train started for Merced, whence the stage starts for the Yosemite Valley. Here I found a good hotel, and, after travelling five nights out of six, I had hoped for a good sleep, though a short one, but my slumbers were disturbed by the plague of mosquitoes.

At six o'clock, on the morning of the 24th, I started in the stage, my companions being two ladies and two gentlemen from Indiana. Crossing an arid plain, where the heat was great, we ascended a little, and came to a village called Hornitos. Soon after this we changed with the up-carriage, which was a great advantage to me, as the previous one had no cover for my head, as I had the box. This, as the temperature was near 90°, was a great improvement. The road is often little more than a track, while the dust is disagreeable, and the jolting tremendous. We lunched at Mariposa, the capital of the district, round which is an enormous estate of sixteen miles square, given by the Government to General Fremont, and sold by him to a company, of whose management I heard great complaints. From Mariposa the road was beautiful, winding through wooded vales and over hills. We surmounted a very long ascent just as it got completely dark, but the negro who drove the stage guided us down a four-mile descent with great dexterity, and about eight o'clock we reached a station called Clark's, in the midst of forests, where two long ranges of wooden rooms, one for living and one for sleeping in, constitute what in such a locality is a comfortable inn. Seeing the Duke of Manchester's photograph on the wall, I found, on inquiry, that he had spent a week here. I found the journey to the Yosemite a longer affair than I had contemplated, and that I could not reach San Francisco till the day before the sailing of the steamer. This was inconvenient, and what added to the inconvenience was that, being misled by an advertisement, I had not allowed for the expense of the trip, and as circular notes are not convertible in these wilds, I had run short of money. This was very unpleasant, particularly in a country where the hotel system does not permit one to economize. However, my landlord, Mr. Moore, whose kindness I gratefully remember, was good enough to give me credit for my bill, which enabled me to scrape through, and I had patiently to submit to the curtailment of my stay in San Francisco.

We went on horseback on the 25th to the Mariposa big trees, and, after ascending through the woods for one hour and a half, we reached what is called the "Fallen Giant," an immense tree stretched along the ground for 208 feet. Proceeding on, we visited others, called the "Grisly Giant," "Ohio," "Indiana," "Illinois," &c. One of them has been found by measurement to be 280 feet high, though Mr. Moore thinks another to be 300. Most of them bear signs of fire, owing to fires kindled sometimes by Indians, sometimes by shepherds, to clear away brushwood. The highest point we reached commanded a very fine view over boundless forests, though one felt the want of water. After leaving Clark's, the road winds over a mountain chain beautifully wooded, and commanding lovely views of rock and dale, and descends into the Yosemite Valley, passing what is called the Bridal Veil Fall.

The valley is situated at a height 4060 feet above the sea, and is surrounded by mountains rising some 4000 or 5000 feet higher. The scenery is magnificent, owing to the bold, precipitous, and rocky character of the mountains, though it is deficient in those features to which the Swiss traveller is accustomed, the glacier and the avalanche. At the time of my visit there had been a long drought, and consequently the Falls were very low. The Yosemite Fall, opposite the village, which in three different cascades descends for 2634 feet, and I fancy must resemble the Reichenbach at Meyringen, was dry, and the Mirror Lake, which is so named from the reflection of the surrounding mountains on its waters, was low. A river, entering the valley, comes down from the rocks above by what is named the Nevada Fall, and a little farther on forms another, called the Vernal—both beautiful.

The valley is quitted on horseback, the tourist rejoining the stage half-way on the road to Clark's. Here every one rides, guides as well as travellers, the former presenting a great contrast to their hardy brethren in Switzerland. The heat of the climate is some excuse for them. The path ascends the mountains at the back of the village, and after a steep climb of two hours and a half, commanding fine views of the valley, reaches Glacier Point (why so named I could not make out, as there is no glacier), whence a splendid view is obtained of the Mirror Lake, the Vernal and Nevada Falls, and the surrounding scenery. We then proceeded to the Sentinel Dome, 8540 feet above the sea, where a magnificent panorama presents itself of rocky mountains and richly-wooded valleys. We rode on through a park-like country which reminded me of the line,—

"O'er California's pathless world of woods,"

to the place where we rejoined the stage. This line of Montgomery's puzzled me a good deal, for though it is appropriate to the hilly region of the Sierra Nevada, yet the coast of California, which was all that was known when the poem was written, is destitute of trees. We saw deer ranging about the forest, and I understand that the poor Indians who are left in these parts hunt them.

On leaving Clark's our party was joined by an engineer engaged on the road, and at Mariposa by a doctor, who complained that practice was so bad in these parts that he could not remain there. After a jolting and hot ride (the thermometer was 92° at 5 p.m.), we reached Merced on the evening of the 29th, and next morning I proceeded by train, through the fertile though arid valley of St. Juan, to Lathrop, on the Central Pacific main line. Merced is a specimen of the way towns spring up in America. It is a new town, and yet it has a good and comfortable hotel, public buildings, and, no doubt, one or more daily newspapers. In America, every little place, instead of depending on the larger cities, starts its own papers. The line from Lathrop crosses some hills, and, passing through a rather pleasing country, reaches Oaklands, opposite San Francisco, with which it is connected by a steam ferry. Unfortunately a sea fog prevented my enjoying what must be a magnificent scene, but I reached my destination and put up at the Occidental Hotel, which struck me as quite as good and a great deal cheaper than the Fifth Avenue at New York. Mr. Snow, a gentleman residing here, with whom I had crossed in the "City of Chester," and his partner, Dr. May, were most kind in showing me about this magnificent city. I had to arrange about my passage, and make preparations for it, after which I took a walk through the noble streets, which are particularly striking when one recollects that the whole place has arisen in little more than thirty years.

In the evening Mr. Snow took me to a great exhibition for California, which was large and very pretty; and next morning showed me over the Palace Hotel, the largest in the world, which was to be opened in a few days, to accommodate 1500 people.[1]

To an Englishman it seems extraordinary how such a gigantic hotel can pay, despite the large number of travellers who visit San Francisco. I believe the

[1] It was opened about a fortnight afterwards.

explanation is to be found in the American habit of residing in hotels. The expense of houses is so great that married couples without encumbrance, or even with small families, find it cheaper and more convenient to patronize these great establishments than to set up for themselves.

I much regretted that want of time, caused by my detention at the Yosemite, prevented my visiting the Chinese quarter, and learning something of the condition of the large Chinese population which inhabits the city. The emigration to California from China is on a very large scale, and, as far as I could learn, is an advantage to both countries. China has an overflowing population, while California and the other Pacific States require labour. In China wages are low; in the Pacific States they are high. Hence it is obviously for the interests of both countries that emigration should go on. After leaving Ogden one meets numerous Chinese. So far as I could learn, they are generally well-conducted, and I heard many people wishing they could get them in the Eastern States, as they make capital servants. Perhaps the climate would be a difficulty, as it is a curious fact that the Northern Chinese never leave their country, and the natives of Canton and Swatow would suffer from the cold winters of New England and New York. They seem to make themselves useful in various capacities—as labourers on the railroads, as household servants, and as traders. Sometimes they accumulate considerable sums, and some of them become very rich. They retain a great love for their native country, and are anxious, when they have saved money, to return to it; but whether they live to revisit it or not, they make arrangements that their bodies should be sent back to be laid in the soil of China. As regards the Chinese town in San Francisco, I apprehend that it much resembles a city in China, though sanitary arrangements and police supervision improve its aspect. Opium-smoking and prostitution abound in it. Perhaps the better class of Chinese, as a rule, proceed up country, while the more dissolute remain in this vast city.

On the morning of Friday, October 1st (afterwards, when we had much head-wind, it was remembered that we sailed on a Friday), I took leave of my kind friend, Mr. Snow, and proceeded in a lumbering coach, which might have been built in the days of Louis XIV., to the wharf of the Pacific Mail Steam Packet Company, where I embarked in the "Alaska," Captain Howard, which started at midday. The fog which prevented my seeing much of the city continued, and we passed through the celebrated Golden Gates, the entrance to the harbour of San Francisco, without being able to see anything of them. This was disappointing in a scene I never expected to see again. At two the pilot left, and we commenced our voyage, the day being cold and misty, but at about half-past five the fog cleared, and we saw the Farralore Islands, or rather rocks, the last vestige of land on the American coast, distinguished by a flashing light. Mr. Schlatter, the doctor of the ship, said, "Take a good look at them, for it is the last land you will see for a month." His words were very unpalatable at the time, but they proved to be true.

I have said nothing of my impressions of the state of affairs in the United States, because I feel that, in hurriedly passing across the continent, without letters of introduction to statesmen and others who could give reliable information, it would be presumption to form an opinion on many interesting questions. I am a Churchman and a Tory; I admire neither the religious nor the political institutions of the Union, and my principles were strengthened by what I saw and heard. It is, however, only right that I should bear my grateful testimony to the courtesy and the kindness I experienced from all with whom I came in contact. The Americans seem very anxious that Englishmen should receive a favourable impression of their country, and often exert themselves to serve them. The only exception I found to this courtesy was not in America, but on board the "City of Chester." A drunken Yankee, soon after leaving Queenstown, began abusing the Prince of Wales. I was obliged to tell him, "You must remember, sir, that I am an Englishman, and if you insult my Prince you insult me." The fellow was rude at the time, but was quiet during the remainder of the voyage.

The "Alaska" is a fine large paddle-wheel steamer, with a beam engine, of about 4000 tons. She is very comfortable, as the cabins are large, the state-rooms good, and there is a deck 115 yards long for exercise. The great apprehension they seem to entertain is fire, against which great precautions are taken. It struck me that these vessels incur risk from their want of power to sail. This is, I believe, the longest voyage taken by steamers, as I am not speaking of sailing-ships with auxiliary screw power. From San Francisco to Yokohama direct is 4700 miles, though by going to the north in a great circle it may be shortened to 4550, but this often takes a boat into heavy weather. In our case, owing to steering south to get into smooth water, the distance traversed was 5060. Now in sailing west, when head-winds are generally encountered, it is very possible that a steamer may run short of coals. Except Honolulu, which is 1500 miles from San Francisco, and off the direct course many hundred miles, there is no port to be gained, and a vessel out of coals, if unable to sail, might be left to float for weeks. On the Atlantic it would not be many days, probably not many hours, before another ship hove in sight, but on the Pacific no help is likely to be at hand. Hence it would seem to be important that a steamer making this long voyage should be able to sail in case of accident, and the White Star boats, which have been chartered to run alternately with the Pacific Mail, are able to do so, as are the new screw-boats the company are building. The old ships, however, depend entirely on coal. I cannot but think that making the passage to the West in them involves a certain amount of risk. Coming East, of course it is different, as the prevailing winds are westerly. It is said that, during several years they have made the voyage, no accident has happened from this cause. Still one can but regard the passage across the Pacific in these boats like an unpleasant fence one has safely ridden over, and I should advise any one going to Yokohama to arrange to take the White Star steamer, unless the screw-vessels, which have been recently built, are by this time repaired and running. The Pacific Mail Company have lately built two splendid screw-steamers, the "City of Pekin" and the "City of Takio," but the contractor so scandalously performed his work that the "Pekin" had to be reconstructed, and the "Takio," in which we were to have sailed, was detained for repairs, though she performed the voyage a month later, and was at Hongkong when I arrived there. We started with 1400 tons of coal, and had 100 left on arrival, but there are several instances of ships being reduced to a very few tons. In one instance they had not ten tons left. The high upper deck, on which several cabins are placed, is a hindrance with adverse winds. The passage is supposed to take from twenty to twenty-five days, but it is oftener the latter than the former. After crossing the Atlantic at the rate of 330 miles a day, one thinks these boats might accomplish 220, but the necessity of husbanding coals for this long voyage over an unfrequented sea often precludes this.

Our company consisted of between thirty and forty cabin passengers, including Captain Von Essendecker, the German Minister at Yeddo, Baron Von Gumschmid, his Secretary of Legation, and Mr. Morton, a lawyer of

Boston. There was a large party of Baptist missionaries proceeding to different places in China and Japan, besides two doctors in the American navy, a barrister of Hongkong, and several "globe-trollers," as those who travel round the world are called in China. On Sundays the service of the American Episcopal Church was read, and Mr. McKippin, a missionary proceeding to Swatow, preached. We had a very large number of Chinese on board; the waiters at dinner, who looked picturesque, were Chinese, the sailors were Chinese, and we had about 800 steerage passengers Chinese. These latter were returning to China with their little fortunes. They are sad gamblers, and, I was told, sometimes lose the whole of their savings in making bets on the day's run. Many of them are addicted to opium-smoking, and frequent the den where it is allowed, which seems always thronged. One of the few women on board came to Captain Howard saying if she did not have opium she should die. He had forbidden her the opium room, but thought himself obliged to allow her to go there for two hours, which time she said she required. The Chinese sleep in the lower part of the ship, and many of them, if permitted, would remain there all day, but the captain finds it necessary to turn them all out for the sake of ventilation. It is on such regulations that the health of ships must greatly depend, and I have been told that sickness generally prevails where captains do not understand the habits of emigrants. The crew is composed of Swatow men. There is such an enmity between the inhabitants of the two districts of Canton and Swatow, that it is thought undesirable to have them together:—

"Est inter finitimos vetus et antiqua simultas."

They, however, resemble each other in being a migratory race, while the inhabitants of Northern China seldom or never leave their country.

On the 2nd, the day after we started, we passed a ship, and on the 7th, Captain Howard thought he saw the smoke of a steamer, supposed to be the "Colorado," the Pacific Mail steamer, bound to San Francisco, in the offing. With this exception we saw nothing but sea-gulls and flying fish during the whole voyage. We were for a long time 1000 to 1500 miles from the nearest land, alone in this vast, solitary ocean. What a comfort is it, under such circumstances, to remember that "The eternal God is our refuge, and underneath are the everlasting arms"!

The first two or three days were fine, and we made about 176 knots a day. It then came on to blow, and though we had not a positive storm, yet we had a great deal of heavy weather with head-winds. Our distance fell day by day, 142, 128, till on the 13th it reached the minimum, 106. In order to get out of head-winds, the captain steered south, and we got as low as latitude 29. This ultimately succeeded, as the weather became calm, but when the change took place, we had drawn so largely on our supply of coals, that he was afraid to put on steam, and we continued to make slow progress. Ultimately he grew more easy on this point, and we made 233 on the 27th, and 236 on the 31st. The average of our thirty days' passage was 168. At sea, the great subject of conversation is the progress made, and people pulled long faces at its slowness. The baron was particularly doleful, talking about eating his Christmas dinner on board the "Alaska." I used to tell him that he, of all people, need not mind, as he would see quite enough of Japan before he left it, while as to some of us, our detention ruined our chance of seeing Pekin.

Soon after three on the 20th, we crossed the parallel of 180° longitude opposite the meridian of Greenwich, and consequently Thursday the 21st was dropped out of our calendar. In going West, each day gets longer than its predecessor by four minutes for every degree you travel. In crossing the Atlantic it is half an hour later; even with our slow progress on the Pacific, a quarter; in crossing the American continent by railway, it is almost an hour. Hence one day gets added on to others. People talk about losing a day, and in the sense that you eat one dinner less in your life you do. In going East it is the reverse. Here each day is shorter than twenty-four hours, according to the distance you travel, and a day has to be intercalated. The time is the reverse of that at Greenwich, midday here being midnight there. As the 180th degree, with the exception of some land in the Arctic regions, passes entirely across the sea, these corrections have always to be made on shipboard.

The views of the ocean by moonlight were very beautiful. Large flocks of gulls followed the ship, and flying fish were often visible. A voyage gives one a good deal of time for reading, and fortunately the "Alaska" had a library on board. Though tedious, I thought myself as well off as if I had been at the seaside. It seems to me quite as pleasant to be enjoying the sea air in a good ship as to be counting the waves at Brighton. At length our long voyage drew to an end. On Sunday the 31st, after service, the distance was posted up as 143 to Yokohama. Several land-birds appeared, driven out by the wind, and settled on the vessel. It blew hard at night, and we were glad that, under the care of a protecting Providence, we were near our destination, and had not to encounter a gale far from land.

CHAPTER II.

EXCURSIONS IN JAPAN.

On coming on deck early on the morning of November 1st, I found the Japanese land before us. The outline of mountains rising to considerable heights, and sinking with wooded sides into the water, with countless white sails of junks in the foreground, constituted a lovely scene, which a month at sea fitted us to enjoy. The sail up the arm of the sea, in which Yokohama is situated, and which extends to Yeddo, is very fine, reminding me of the entrance to Plymouth Sound.

At twelve o'clock, after a passage of thirty days, six hours, twenty-eight minutes, we anchored opposite the beautiful town of Yokohama, in a harbour filled with men-of-war and ships of various nations, when I took leave of Captain Howard and the "Alaska,"

> "Though lost to sight, to memory dear,"

as the baron said of her, and once more set foot on *terra firma*.

I established myself at the Grand Hotel—a very comfortable house—managed by a company, of which Mr. Smith, a gentleman whose public spirit has done much for Yokohama, and to whose courtesy and knowledge of Japan travellers who consult him are much indebted, is a leading director. There are several other hotels in the town. The first thing which strikes one on landing is the jinrikisha, the conveyance of the country, which is a seat placed on wheels, and drawn by one or, for longer distances, two men, who run along, sometimes going as much as seven miles an hour. It is comfortable, though for my part I do not like turning men into cattle. In the afternoon I paid a visit to Yeddo, returning to Yokohama to dinner. The distance of nearly twenty miles is accomplished by a railway, recently constructed, which runs at a little distance from the shores of the gulf, through fields of rice, passing several villages. The snowy mass of Fusiama, the great volcano of Japan, rising to the height of nearly 13,000 feet, looks very striking from the line. My object in going at once to Yeddo was to consult Sir Harry Parkes, the British Minister there, as to the possibility of visiting Pekin. He very kindly considered the question, and told me, unless I was prepared to give up seeing Japan and to proceed at once to China, I could not attempt it. I felt that it would be most unwise to hurry on, and therefore abandoned the idea of Pekin. I found afterwards that those who arrived three weeks earlier thought themselves too late to attempt it.

It is curious to have been cut off from all communication with the world for a month. On the day we left San Francisco a telegram appeared in the papers, copied from the *Times* of the same morning, which the eight hours' difference in time admits, giving a most alarming account of the complications in connexion with Herzegovina. On arriving in Japan, our first question was whether there was any news from Turkey, and whether war had broken out; and we were surprised to learn that the question continued *in statu quo*. Next day I again visited Yeddo and took tiffin, as lunch is called in the East, with Sir Harry and Lady Parkes, where I met Baron Struve, the Russian Minister, who was just removing his head-quarters from Yokohama to Yeddo, as most of his diplomatic brethren have done before him. Yeddo, or Tokio, as it is sometimes called, meaning Eastern capital, as distinguished from Kioto, the Western capital, was long the capital of the Tycoons, and is now of the Emperors. The idea used to prevail that the temporal sovereign of Japan, called Tycoon or Shogun, ruled at Tokio, while the Mikado, or spiritual potentate, reigned at Kioto. This idea turned out to be unfounded. The state of Japan, twenty years since, presented many analogies to the state of Europe in the dark ages. The Mikado was a *roi fainéant*, like the Merovingians or later Carlovingians, though, being supposed by the people to be the Son of the Gods, he could not be dethroned. He resided in stately seclusion in his palace at Kioto, surrounded by courtiers and concubines. The Shogun, at Tokio, was the mayor of the palace and the general of the kingdom, while the great Daimios, or native princes, answered to the feudal nobles. The jealousy between the Shogun and the Daimios was constant; and to secure his power the former compelled the latter to reside at Tokio, or, if absent at their estates, to leave their wives and children as hostages. The Daimios were in the habit of maintaining large bodies of armed retainers, soldiers carrying two swords, whose lawless excesses were the terror of the people. It was remarkable that the nominal and the real power often resided in different hands by a system of regents. The Mikado was frequently a child under a guardian. So also was the Shogun; so, too, some of the chief Daimios. The nominal rulers, if not minors, were too often sunk in sensuality and sloth, and ambitious men wielded power in their names. Iyeyas, the founder of the last dynasty of Shoguns, who, by his genius and valour, raised himself above his fellow-daimios to the government of the kingdom, must have been a great man; but it was impossible that his descendants, during nearly three centuries, should retain his abilities, though the last Tycoon, who is now living in retirement, appears to have been worthy of a better fate. The wonder seems to be that the Shoguns should have resisted the intrigues of their rivals for so long a period; but the forced entrance of foreigners into the country precipitated a revolution, which could hardly have been much longer delayed. The Daimios overcame the Tycoons. The Mikado, who is now called the Emperor, removed from Kioto to Tokio, and the administration is carried on in his name, though, as he is very young, and said to be deficient in ability, the great struggle is to get possession of his person. Sanjo, formerly a retainer of one of the great houses, has for some years carried on the government, though, at the moment of my visit, Saburo, the chief of the great clan of Satsuma, was making an effort to displace him. What is very remarkable is that the great Daimios have quietly given up their armed retainers, and the carrying of arms is now prohibited. The disarmament of these samurai or two-sworded men has greatly conduced to the peace of the country, though how to provide for them is one of the great difficulties of the time—a difficulty which may perhaps force Japan into war.

After tiffin I visited Sheva, the last resting-place of many of the Tycoons. This collection of tombs and temples spreads over a considerable space. The temples are not large, but very ornate, presenting a contrast to the size and interior plainness of Mohammedan mosques. I ascended what are called the 100 steps, though they are really more, to a terrace commanding a full view over Yeddo. The vast city, situated on the shores of its gulf, stretches away towards the East till it is lost in the distance. Its large scattered buildings and wide streets are estimated to contain 800,000 people. On the other side the sun was sinking behind the snow of Fusiama. I thought it had just risen in dear old England. I returned to Yokohama third class, which gave me an opportunity of seeing something of the lower class of Japanese. From the loose-flowing robes of both sexes it is difficult to distinguish the men from the women. The men shave part of their heads, and wear the rest of their hair in a knot. The upper classes wear European dress, though Saburo and the party which he leads retain the national costume. The people smoke very small pipes of tobacco, which constantly require refilling. The use of opium is unknown here. The 3rd, being the Emperor's birthday, was observed in European fashion by reviews, illuminations, and dinners. I took an early tiffin with Mr. Kingdon, a merchant who lives on the Bluff—a plateau overlooking the town, where most Europeans reside. I met a party who were going to the Yokohama races, the first institution which Western civilization introduced into Japan.

After tiffin I started on an expedition to the Hills, under a Government passport procured for me by Sir Harry Parkes. No foreigner is allowed to go beyond certain limits fixed by treaty without permission from the Japanese Government, which is given on the application of the Minister of the nation to which he belongs. It is one of the remarkable circumstances connected with Japan that whereas within a few years the Ministers of the Treaty Powers lived in fear of their lives, one can now travel through the whole country without the smallest apprehension. On my saying to Mr. Smith that I supposed I might walk about Yokohama as freely as I might about London, he replied, "Yes, with this difference, that in London you might lose your watch; in Yokohama you won't." Some people advised me to take an interpreter, but the one who was recommended to me was engaged, and I therefore trusted to signs and the few words of English which my jinrikisha men knew. I always think *valets de place* a nuisance in all countries, and having made my way from St. Petersburg to Sebastopol with no knowledge of Russian, except the numbers and the important word "skolko" (how much), I had come to the conclusion that it is easier to get along in a strange language than is generally supposed. Lady Parkes remarked to me, on my return, that the Japanese were always very kind to those who went without servants, and so I found it. I had a good-sized jinrikisha, with a head in case of rain, two men who went for a dollar a day each, and a basket of provisions, as the native inns or tea-houses only produce eggs, rice, and fish. Leaving Yokohama about two o'clock, we passed through some pretty valleys, chiefly producing rice, and at length began to ascend. The day was unfortunately rather wet, but, on reaching the summit of the pass, a lovely prospect over hill and woodland, with some fine islands in the sea in the background, met the eye. We descended to Kanasawa, beautifully situated at the head of a gulf, and proceeded to Kamakura, the capital of this part of Japan before the Tycoons built Yeddo. It is now merely a collection of scattered hamlets, though, when the Jesuits visited it in the sixteenth century, they estimated the population at

200,000. Here I stopped at the Japanese tea-house, one of the houses of the village turned into an inn. It was built with sliding panels between the rooms, and if the people were not honest you would be easily robbed, as it would be impossible to lock yourself in. Japanese houses are well described by Baron Von Hubner in his "Ramble round the World," who says, "The temples, castles, palaces, middle-class houses, and poor cottages are all composed of the same elements—a flooring raised a certain number of feet above the soil (which is a necessary precaution against damp and reptiles), then four or more vertical beams and a heavy roof. The partition walls are only frames covered with paper running in a groove. The outside wall is replaced by wooden shutters, fastened during the night. In the temples, castles, and yashkis there is besides a real wall of stone covered with cement. All the rest is in wood. It is the most primitive construction possible, and at the same time the most suited to the climate, and to the financial position of the nation. It resists earthquakes and typhoons infinitely better than the stone houses of the Europeans. It is more exposed to the danger of fire; but even if injured or destroyed by fire, wind, or the earth's convulsions, the evil is remedied both promptly and easily."

In such a house I for the first time dined and slept. On my return to Yokohama I heard that two shocks of an earthquake were felt during this night. Whether they did not extend to Kamakura, or whether I slept too sound to notice them, I do not know, but I felt nothing of them. Earthquakes are frequent here, though I should think hardly so frequent as at San Francisco. Next morning I visited the great temple of Kamakura, dedicated to Shinto. It is a fine specimen of a Japanese temple, with a grove of trees leading to it. Here several curious relics of the history of Japan are shown. It is remarkable as the scene of the murder of Sanitomo, the last Shogun of the line of Yoritomo. About a mile further on we came to Dar Butsn, the great statue of Budda. According to a statement placed there, it is 144 feet high, and 87 feet in circumference; the length of the eyes is 3½ feet, that of the ears 6 feet, the width of the mouth 3 feet, the circumference of the thumb 3½ feet, and that of the leg 34 feet. Inside it is a sort of chapel. It reminded me of the Sphinx; but it enjoys the advantage of sitting in solitary grandeur, while the Egyptian monster suffers by comparison with its gigantic neighbours the Pyramids. I gave up visiting the island of Yenosima, needlessly as I afterwards found, and proceeded through pretty valleys with a fine view of Fusiama to Fujisawa, where we joined the Tokaido, the great road of Japan. This road runs from one end of the island to the other, and does great credit to Japanese energy. It is the route from Tokio to Kioto. Passing a succession of populous towns we reached Odawara, the chief city of these parts, situated on the sea. Here my men wanted to stop, but, following the paper of instructions I had, I insisted on going on; and it was well I did so, as the following day was sufficiently long. Leaving the jinrikisha, as the mountain path was impracticable for wheels, we walked six miles to Hata. Leaving the Bay of Odawara, we began to ascend through lovely valleys, passing the village of Yamoto. Near this the road terminated, and was succeeded by a path of great stone boulders which would be difficult for horses. The walk was beautiful, but it grew dark, except the light of a young moon, about an hour before we reached Hata. Here it was with some difficulty we got taken in, but I managed to get what I wanted—a room to lie down in. On the morning of the 5th, sending one of my men back with my things to Odawara, I started with the other as guide for Hakone. From Hata to Hakone is four miles, and from Hakone, by Myanoshila, to Oduwara is fourteen. After reaching the summit of the pass, which reminds one of Switzerland, the Lake of Hakone comes in view, with Fusiama in the distance, presenting a beautiful scene, though the hills round are barren. Descending through woods the path goes round the end of the lake to the village of Hakone, beyond which one sees the Tokaido, marked by telegraph poles, winding its way to Kioto. I ought to have taken a boat on the lake, but from not speaking the language, I failed to arrange for one. I therefore retraced my steps, and after visiting the deserted temples of Mota Hakone, situated amid lovely woods on the shores of the lake, I reascended to the pass, and, turning to the left, passed over a desolate mountain tract with two small lakes, where were some figures either of Shinto or Budda, and descended to the village of Ashinoya.

As we descended further we came into wooded valleys and reached the beautiful village of Myanoshita, celebrated for its hot baths. The walk from here to Yamoto is lovely. The path descends through woods with a stream murmuring below, reminding me of the most beautiful valleys of the Alps. At the pretty village of Togi Sani the stream is reached, and the path lies along its banks to Yamoto, shortly after which place it joins that to Hata amid striking scenery. My jinrikisha met me some three miles from Odawara, which possesses an inn of some pretensions, as it has beds without sheets and rooms without panels.

Next day I returned along the Tokaido. During this excursion I have been entirely among the Japanese, with no one with whom I could converse, which has given me the opportunity of watching the life of the lower classes. I was very much struck with the large population. Never, except near populous cities, have I seen such a succession of houses without intermission. This explains the figures of the official census of 1872, which fixes the entire population at 33,110,825. In some respects they are a very primitive people, and the dress of both sexes, when at work, is very scanty. On the other hand, their streets are very clean. The men go through immense labour, running with horses and jinrikishas, and carrying burdens, while the women, and sometimes quite little girls, carry heavy children, slung in their cloaks behind their backs. There seems little religion among them, for, though the temples are numerous, there are hardly any worshippers. It was my first visit to a heathen land, and contrasting these people with the inhabitants of Turkey, Syria, and Egypt, made me think that the absence of idolatry places the Mohammedans, with all their errors, in a far superior position to the worshippers of idols. It made me feel the immense importance of Christian missions in Japan. We have forced our way into the country, but Europeans too often imitate the vices and the immorality of the natives; and unless we give them the Bible, we shall have done them harm instead of good. Our route was along the Tokaido, which, after leaving Fujisawa, passes through pretty valleys, which lead down to the plain in which Yokohama is situated. The 7th was Sunday, and for the second time since leaving home I was glad to be able to attend church, which was very full. Before evening service I took a walk on the Bluff, which commands charming views over the gulf. The "Oceanic," the White Star boat, which left San Francisco on the 16th, arrived at midday, thus gaining nine days on the "Alaska." She went the northern course of only 4500 miles, though she had encountered some heavy weather.

On the 8th I visited Yeddo, to give up my pass for Hakone, as the Japanese Government expect passes to be returned after the journey is accomplished, to ask for one for Kioto, and to take leave of Sir H. and Lady Parkes, who had been most kind to me. It is a great advantage to the interests of England to have at Yeddo a statesman of the talents, experience, and knowledge of the East possessed by Sir Harry Parkes, while the services he has rendered to Japan by his exertions to promote the morality and improvement of the people deserve to be gratefully remembered. In a country which in a few years has shaken off the system which has prevailed for ten centuries, and is now striving to enter on a course of imitation of Western civilization, it is of immense importance that the representatives of the Great Powers should act with wisdom, and therefore it is of the utmost consequence to Great Britain that her minister should be a man who can maintain her influence. In the evening Baron Von Gumschmid, who was settling into his duties at the German Legation, dined with me. I was much indebted to his conversation for whiling away time during our long and tedious voyage.

I devoted next day to a stroll through Yeddo, which is situated on a gulf so wide that the opposite shore is lost in the distance. The grounds of the castle, formerly occupied by the Tycoon, and now by the Emperor, take up a very large space; and there are, besides, several castles of Daimios, who were forced to reside there by the jealousy of the Shoguns. I walked up the principal street, visiting an exhibition of Japanese curiosities, and a show of monkeys, which seemed to amuse the people. One seems in a thoroughly foreign land. The dark-coloured population of both sexes, with their curious head-gear and loose-flowing robes, the Buddhist priests, with their completely shaven heads, yellow dresses, the innumerable jinrikishas, the grooms running in attendance on their horses, make up a striking scene. The women here move about as freely as they do in Europe—a great contrast to Mohammedan countries. Whether for semi-civilized countries the Mohammedan plan is not the best is a point which may well be doubted. After seeing a temple which has been turned into a library, I reached a plateau, covered with woods, with several very fine temples interspersed among them. It seemed a place of great resort to the inhabitants of Yeddo. One of these temples, which were much ornamented, seemed filled with worshippers. It was the first time I had seen any evidence of superstitious feeling on the part of the Japanese, who struck me as a people destitute of all religion. It seems as though infidelity was on the increase here, as in many other parts of the world. I recollect the celebrated traveller, Captain Speke, whose melancholy fate caused such general grief, telling me that among the savage tribes among whom he travelled, what he called "Colensoism" was making great progress. It would seem, in like manner, that the Japanese are losing belief in their old religions. God grant they may find the true faith! In the evening, in company with Mr Otto, one of my companions in the "Alaska," I went to a Japanese theatre. The performance goes on from the afternoon till late in the night. The people seemed much to enjoy it, and according to appearance it was very decently conducted. Whether the language was obscene I of course could not judge; but the conversation of the lower classes is said to be very disgusting.

On the 10th I took my passage for Shanghai, with

permission to stop at Kobe, for sixty-five dollars. Till within the last few weeks the American Company, the Pacific Mail, had been running in opposition to the Mitsu Bishi, the Japanese Company, and the fares had been very low—I think only twenty dollars from Yokohama to Shanghai. Hence passengers were advised at San Francisco not to book beyond Yokohama; but while we were on the Pacific the Japanese bought up the American boats, and raised the charge to sixty-five dollars. At this there was much grumbling, though, compared with other fares in the Chinese seas, it did not seem excessive. The currency in Japan is in a curious position, as all payments are made in Japanese notes (down to ten cents). As these are printed in Chinese characters, it takes a good deal of trouble to learn the different descriptions. From all I could gather, finance is the great difficulty of Japan, as of many other countries. Now, we know that when finances are bad, and cash payments suspended, gold is always at a premium. Such, at the present moment, is the case in Russia, Austria, Italy, and the United States. In the course of my journey, gold was seventeen premium in New York, and seven in Italy, where I had known it ten barely twelve months before. What struck me as extraordinary in Japan was, that, with the finances in a critical position, and cash payments suspended, gold commanded no premium—in fact, was at a small discount. The people seemed to prefer paper. On the day of my landing I tendered at the railway station a Mexican dollar as the fare to Yeddo. The clerk did not evidently like it; but, as we spoke no language in common, he at length received it. On my inquiring about this at the hotel, they told me he would make a loss, though almost infinitesimal, on my dollar. Before starting for Hakone, as I was going where I had little means of communication, I was anxious to lay in a stock of Yens (paper dollars), Bus (quarter dollars), and lesser notes; but these were procured for me with some difficulty, and at a premium. This extravagant fondness for paper is different from anything I ever experienced elsewhere. I had a curious walk through the town, endeavouring to find Mr. Kingdon's office. The houses were numbered in a way I could not comprehend, and my inquiries, which I had been instructed to make for Kingdon Sah, were of no avail. At length I found a shop with "cordonnier" over it, and I accosted a civil shopkeeper in French, but found him glad to exchange it for Italian, though, in reply to my remark that he was an Italian, he said, "Io sono Francese." The French are not a travelling people, and one very rarely meets them here. I lunched at the hotel with Mr. Morton, who had crossed in the "Alaska,"—a very superior man, but an intense American. He seemed to think that Japan might become a State of the Union. I told him that a semi-barbarous people required to be governed, and that they seemed to me utterly unfitted for the advanced institutions of the States.

In the afternoon I left the Grand Hotel, where I had

been very comfortable, and embarked on board the steamer "Golden Age," Captain Furber, which, since it has changed hands, rejoices in a Japanese name. We were a large company, including several of my fellow-passengers who were proceeding to Shanghai, while many of the inhabitants of Yokohama came to see us off. The afternoon was wet and misty, which spoiled the beauty of the sail down the gulf. Next day was fine, though the morning was very rough, and as the land trends in we seemed to be far out at sea. In the afternoon we were again near land, and enjoyed a very beautiful sail as long as daylight lasted. Though the Japanese have purchased the Pacific Mail boats, they have to leave the American captains and officers in charge. This they are compelled to do, as otherwise the underwriters would refuse to insure. Captain Furber has a great reputation for his knowledge of these dangerous seas.

On waking on the morning of the 12th I found we were at anchor in the harbour of Kobe. The houses of Hiogo and Kobe are built along the shore, and join each other like Hastings and St. Leonards. Hiogo is the treaty port, and the consuls are described as consuls at Hiogo; but their residences, together with those of the leading merchants, are at Kobe, which is a very pretty seaside town. Leaving the "Golden Age," and breakfasting at Mrs. Green's Hiogo Hotel, I proceeded, without loss of time, by railway to Osaka. The line first skirts the beautiful gulf, and then runs through a plain (inland). I was told that the Japanese have been much swindled about their railways, which have cost 30,000*l.* a mile, though the country is easy for their construction. It is intended to continue this line from Osaka to Kioto, which will be a great convenience to future travellers, who, by making the most of their time, will be able to see Kioto during the day that the steamer remains at Kobo, and resume their voyage. At present a visit to Kioto involves a detention of a week. At Osaka I took a jinrikisha and two men, who went tandem, while those I took to Hakoni had gone, one drawing, one helping behind. The charge for these journeys is about one dollar each man a day. Universal as jinrikishas now are even in parts of Japan where foreigners are unknown, they are of very recent introduction, and seven years ago were unheard of. The old national conveyances were norimons and congos. The norimon is a sort of cage, very small to contain a human being, slung on a pole, and carried by two men. The congo is a wooden bed, in the form of a hammock, similarly slung and carried. The road from Osaka to Kioto lies along the banks of the Yodogawa, which is crossed by a ferry in the course of the journey. The distance is thirty-two miles; but the ride is a dull one, as there is no scenery, except distant hills. The cleanliness of the Japanese towns and villages is remarkable, and contrasts favourably with more civilized countries—notably with France. At Fujimi the river is left, and one turns into the plain in which Kioto is situated. My men stopped about nightfall at a place where a curious collection of temples stood among gardens. It was quite dark when we entered Kioto, where I stopped at an inn, which, though it provided an elaborate cuisine, had the Japanese characteristics of wooden walls and sliding panels, which, as the weather was cold, were not conducive to comfort. Moreover, though they professed to speak English, it was of the most meagre description. The people warm themselves over small charcoal hand stoves. The hotel is close to the Gion temple, and at night I saw a Japanese haranguing a crowded audience in a room connected with the temple. The people here seemed to show much more respect for religion than those farther East. Next day I walked to Oats, on Lake Bīwa (pronounced Bīva), situated three ris, or seven miles and a half, from Kioto. Leaving the town by the Tokaido, the great road from Yeddo, I crossed a chain of hills, and came down into another plain, also surrounded by lovely hills. After traversing this plain the road ascends a beautiful pass, and then descends to Oats, a large Japanese town, which is situated at the corner of the lake, a large sheet of water with a plain on one side, but with volcanic mountains in all directions around. There are steamers on Lake Biwa; but, so far as I could ascertain, as I could find no one who spoke more than a few words of English, none crossed and returned during the day, so I abandoned, with regret, the idea of a voyage upon it. After lunching at a tea-house on some cake and Japanese wine, called sakki, I retraced my steps, visiting some temples and cemeteries to the north of Kioto. After dinner I took a stroll through the city, and as it was full moon I had the pleasure—

"To see it by moonlight, when mellowly shines
The light o'er its palaces, gardens, and shrines."

The 14th was Sunday. It felt solemn to spend a solitary Sabbath in the midst of this vast heathen city. May God in His great mercy speedily send the Gospel to it! After reading the Church service, I took a long ramble through the town, which gave me a general idea of it preliminary to Monday, which I devoted to sight-seeing.

Kioto is situated in a large plain, on all sides surrounded by hills. The town is on the western side, and the hill behind it commands a very fine view. This hill is covered with beautiful woods, and appeared to be the site for tea-gardens. The inscription over one of these was in English, or an attempt at it, announcing:—

"ARTIFICIAL WARM MINERAL SPRING
PRINCIPALLIJ CONTAINING
FERRI CARBONAS."

Around the town are rice-fields, the common feature of Japan. These rice-fields require constant irrigation, which one would think was unhealthy, though the people do not appear to suffer from it. The sewage is carefully preserved for manure for the land. I visited a great idol called Darbutz, which consisted of an enormous head, I should think twenty to twenty-five feet high, placed in a temple. I had not access to figures, but it did not strike me as being as large as the idol at Kamakura. Close by is a very curious temple called Sanji

Sanguento. A great idol sits on a throne with a small head over the great head, four other smaller ones in the coronet, and twenty-four hands. Immediately around twenty-six devilish-looking figures are grouped, while in long rows on either side, 1000 other figures are placed, in an attitude of devotion, the latter of a not unpleasing aspect. It is a remarkable and melancholy exhibition of idolatry. The great Buddhist temple of Nishihan-guan-ji is a collection of several buildings which are good specimens of Japanese temples, ornate, but not very large. The interiors reminded me of those of the Greek Churches in Russia. I visited a large number of other temples, of which the city seems full. At the hotel they had put down Gosha, the Mikado's Palace, on my list to be visited, but, on arriving there, a difficulty was made at admitting me, and my jinrikisha men took me to the government office toprocure an order. Here a curious scene presented itself, which a good deal puzzled me, but which I afterwards found was the distribution of prizes for a recent exhibition. Long rows of girls gorgeously dressed, with painted faces, were being marched in procession through the court and about the building, while Japanese gentlemen in European evening dress were directing the proceedings. At length I found the official who had charge of Gosha, who told me I could not see it that day, as it was a holiday, but I might next morning before my return to Hiogo. He was very civil, and sent one of his clerks, who spoke English, to show me everything. This shows the rapid change in Japan, as only four years previously

Baron Von Hubner, accompanied by Mr. Enslie, the British Vice-Consul at Osaka, had the greatest difficulty in obtaining the entrance which is now given as a matter of course to every traveller. The palace is more curious than beautiful. It consists of interminable small rooms separated by sliding panels with paintings on the screens. The only room of any size is the hall in which the Mikados were crowned. The gardens would be pretty if they were kept in order, but they are much neglected, as since the removal of the emperor to Yeddo, he has never paid a visit here. Those who now rule in his name seem so afraid of losing their influence that they discourage his travelling, and he remains as constantly at Tokio as his ancestors did at Kioto. Near Gosha is the palace of the ex-Mikados, who have been numerous in history, as it was not uncommon for princes to abdicate in favour of a child and continue to govern. The young Japanese who accompanied me said the population of Kioto was 600,000. Many Europeans are resident here in the service of the Government.

After leaving Gosha I proceeded to Fujimi, the port of Kioto, where I embarked on board a curious little steamer to descend the Yodi-gawa to Osaka. The voyage was amusing, as the cabin was very small, and I sat in the stern, contemplating the native travellers squatting on the floor. They were very kind, and invited me to share their food. The earlier part of the sail down this fine wide river is beautiful from the mountain views in the distance, though afterwards it becomes dull. The voyage is not without risk, as the steamers are of the worst description, and the bed of the river is very shifting, so that we twice ran aground. The native boats, with their large tattered sails, are picturesque. In four hours and a half we reached Osaka, whence the railway took me to the Hiogo Hotel, Kobe, glad to be again among those with whom I could converse, for though they were very civil and obliging at the "Nakamaraya Higashi Nikonchaya, adjoining the Gien Temple" (I quote the description given on the card, whatever the Japanese words may mean), yet they spoke too little English to make my stay there pleasant. At the hotel I met Dr. Hill and Mr. Marshall, the assistant architect for Government buildings in Japan and China. Dr. Hill is a naval surgeon placed by our Government here to enable the Japanese to carry out the Contagious Diseases Acts, of which we used to hear so much in the last Parliament. I used to vote against them on the good old Tory principle that "what is morally wrong cannot be politically right," and I could not persuade myself that by those Acts a national sanction is not given to vice. At the same time many of those whose opinions I esteem above my own, maintain that no such sanction is given, and those who have come practically in contact with the working of the Acts testify to the beneficial results arising from them. Such was the opinion I heard expressed in Japan, China, and India.[1] In Japan, prostitution pre-

[1] It is only fair to state that in India complaint is made by the natives that the Acts have been repeatedly enforced against innocent women; and I fear it is only too probable that not a

vails to a fearful extent, and obtrudes itself in a way I never witnessed elsewhere, unless, alas! I must except the Haymarket. The chief virtue of the people often leads to this vice. Implicit obedience to parents is the characteristic of the Japanese. Hence, when a girl is ordered by her parents to enter a house of ill-fame, she is bound by her religion to obey, and many men subsist on the wages of their daughters' dishonour. It is stated on the other hand that when these women marry, which they generally ultimately do, they lead virtuous lives, and the fact that the population appears to increase largely seems to show that the conduct of the people is not so bad as one might think. When women marry, they have a curious habit of blackening their teeth.

On the 17th and 18th, I made excursions to Osaka and Arumah. Osaka being united to Kobe, like Yeddo to Yokohama, by railway, the easiest plan is to take up one's quarters at an hotel by the sea, and run over for the day. It is an enormous city, finely situated on a large river, which divides into numerous branches. The number of bridges is consequently very large. The streets present the same aspects of Japanese life as those of Kioto and Tokio, but it is not distinguished by the large buildings and curious temples of the two capitals. The excursion to Arumah requires a jinrikisha and two coolies. The day was fine, though colder than it had been, the autumn tints lovely, and the road,

few virtuous members of the weaker sex have been confounded with a vicious class.

which winds over hills and through wooded valleys, good for horses and jinrikishas, though not fit for carriages. The distance is sixteen miles. Arumah which is very beautifully situated in a valley, is celebrated for sulphur baths, and for the manufacture of curious baskets and boxes. I invested in some of these, but being rather fragile, it was one of the difficulties of my journey to get them home, a difficulty which I surmounted, thanks to the kindness of Captain Anderson, of the "Golconda," and of Mr. Parsons, a fellow-passenger in the "Peshawur." I returned by the same beautiful road, accomplishing the journey in three hours instead of four, owing to going down hill.

On the morning of the 19th the steamer "Genke Maru," late "Costa Rica," Captain Connor, arrived, bringing several passengers who had been on board the "Alaska." I established myself on board her, but took tiffin and dinner with Mr. and Mrs. Annesley, who were very hospitable. Mr. Annesley is H.M.'s consul at Hiogo and previously held the same position at Nagasaki. Early next morning the "Costa Rica" started, and began to pass the lovely inland sea, an arm of the sea dividing the principal island of Niphen from the southern one of Kiushiu. It is a constant succession of islands, promontories, and gulfs. Here it widens into a broad and extensive lake; there it narrows into a contracted channel surrounded by noble hills. The scenes it presents are varied and beautiful, at times reminding me of the Straits of Bonifacio or the Bosphorus, at others of the Italian lakes. For its long succession of varied marine scenery, I have never seen anything like it. Night came on in the midst of this scene, but Captain Connor told us for our comfort that the sail during the night was less interesting. On the morning of the 21st we found ourselves in the Straits of Simonosaki, one of the finest parts of the inland sea, where some years ago an attack was made by our fleet. I was unable to land, as this is not a treaty port, and I had returned my Kioto passport (which could not, moreover, have availed me here) to Sir H. Parkes through Mr. Annesley. These passport regulations seem foolish and vexatious, and can hardly last should travelling increase. Travellers coming to Japan from Shanghai are unable to visit Kioto, unless they have written before to Yeddo to ask the British minister to forward a passport to Kobe. At Simonosaki is the southern termination of the Tokaido, or great Japanese road, which I have had occasion more than once to mention. It runs from here to the northern end of the island, passing there Kioto and Yeddo. It is a work which reflects much honour on the administrations of former days. Similar roads traverse the smaller islands of Yesso and Kinshin. After contemplating the lovely harbour and pretty town for some hours from the deck of our ship, we left about one, and after about five miles quitted the inland sea. The panorama of mountains, woods, and rocky islands was exceedingly fine, reminding me of the coast of Corsica.

The southern portion of Japan is the home of the

great clans of Satsuma, Choshiu, Toza, and Hizen. The condition of this country till the recent revolution must have had many points of resemblance with that of the Highlands in the last century, with which we are familiar from the writings of Scott. The clans were governed by their chiefs, like the Camerons and Grahams of former days, though the jealousy of the Tycoons compelled these chiefs to spend much of their time in Yeddo. Now, by a remarkable change, these Daimios have resigned their power and disbanded their retainers, receiving a fixed income in exchange. Some think this was an ingenious manœuvre on the part of the great Daimios to depress their less powerful brethren, and that the influence of the principal chiefs is as great as ever. The Daimios are said to be satisfied, and some of them may prefer a certain income and greater liberty to their former precarious revenue and splendid slavery to the Tycoons. Still one can hardly think that the more able and ambitious spirits among them can be satisfied to abandon power to the coterie who, for the most part originally dependents of the great houses, now govern in the name of the Emperor. But what may ultimately prove a great difficulty is the discontent of the samurai, the former military retainers of the Daimios. A large body of disbanded soldiers is a curse to any country, and if, as I was told, these men have been very inadequately compensated, and have therefore just ground for dissatisfaction, they may hereafter prove a great hindrance to the tranquillity of the Japanese empire.

We continued our voyage along the coast of the southern island, reaching Nagasaki during the night. The coasts of Japan are well lighted, as the Japanese appointed an English engineer, Mr. Brandon, C.E., to plan and superintend their lighthouses. He was at this time about to return home, and was making a final inspection in company with Sir H. Parkes. On board the steamer was a very intelligent scientific traveller, in the service of the Russian Government, a great grandson of the celebrated Marshal Barclay de Tolly, who had been travelling seventeen years and had seen much of Central Asia. He told me that the journey overland from Pekin to St. Petersburg is now difficult, but that railways are being constructed through Siberia which will greatly expedite it. There was also on board a young lieutenant in the Japanese navy, a Mr. Konrooka, who had studied at Portsmouth, and seemed unceasing in his endeavours to acquire professional and other useful knowledge. He was very busy translating into Japanese the English Articles of War, and applied to me to know the meaning of "property, matter, or thing," in the Act of Parliament, which I told him was legal surplusage.

The "Costa Rica" remained at Nagasaki over the 22nd, and I was most kindly entertained by the Consul and Mrs. Flowers. Nagasaki is a land-locked harbour, the entrance being protected by a long mountainous island. Near this is the rock of Papenburg, whence, in 1638, 4000 Christians were precipitated into the sea. These martyrs were the last remains of the

Church founded in Japan by St. Francis Xavier, and their destruction expelled Christianity from Japan. The town rises very prettily from the shore amid a panorama of exquisite hills, woods, and valleys. From one of these hills behind the town, commanding a splendid view of the magnificent harbour and neighbouring creeks, the Americans observed the transit of Venus. Decima, the old Dutch factory, is a little island, about 300 yards long by 100 yards wide, surrounded on two sides by the harbour, and on the other two by a stinking ditch. Here, up to 1856, the Dutch merchants lived imprisoned, being only allowed once a year to take a walk on the mainland under the care of a guard. It must have been a dreadful life, but by such sacrifices they procured for Holland a monopoly of the trade of Japan. The native town of Nagasaki is celebrated for porcelain and tortoise-shell. Mr. Flowers speaks of the Japanese as a very industrious and fairly honest people. Though they grow so much rice, it is too dear for the lowest class, who chiefly live on barley. The government is a complete system of centralization, and all local affairs are managed from Yeddo, where they are introducing the Code Napoleon. The old samurai, or two-sworded men, have been disarmed, and are now seldom seen. We went to a croquet party at a beautiful place overlooking the harbour, belonging to Mr. Glover, a merchant here, where we met the Hon. Commander Dawson, of H.M. gun-boat "Dwarf," who afterwards dined at the Consul's. His brother, who accompanied him, told me he was twenty-seven days crossing the Pacific in perfectly calm weather. After a pleasant day, I returned to the "Costa Rica," which sailed at midnight. A good lighthouse guided us out of the harbour, though the bright torches burnt by some fishing-boats looked to me very confusing. In the morning we were off Goito, the last island, and about 10 a.m. we passed the "Asses' Ears" and "Palace Rocks," the last rocks of Japan, thus losing sight of these interesting islands.

It has been remarked that Japan is the only nation which has "ever taken ten centuries at a bound." A people just rising from what one of their own ministers called "a sleep of a thousand years" is one of the most remarkable spectacles the world has ever presented. The question suggests itself, whether the recent changes are signs of permanent and satisfactory progress, or merely the prelude of confusion and anarchy. Twenty years ago Japan was in much the same condition as it had remained in for centuries. The Mikado lived in splendid seclusion, but his name was a talisman to rouse the affectionate loyalty of the people. The Shogun, ruling in the name of the Mikado, wielding the military power of the State, administered the resources of the empire. The Daimios, each in their own spheres, exercised great influence, and shared their revenues, chiefly paid in rice, among large bodies of military retainers. The official religion was Shintoism, which represents the Mikado as the descendant of the gods; but a large part of the population were attached to the worship of Buddha. The mass of the people appear to have been orderly, industrious, and contented. The land was well cultivated and productive, while in some of the arts of life they excelled, and their silks, embroidery, porcelain, bronzes, and artistic work in metals, competed with the productions of the Western world. Such was the state of the country when first visited by Europeans. Has its material prosperity been improved by contact with Western civilization? The *auri sacra fames* impelled commerce to Japan. In 1854 two ports were thrown open to the ships and merchants of the United States, England, and Russia; and in 1858 Lord Elgin and Baron Gros, flushed with a recent victory over the Chinese, concluded treaties which opened Japan to the commerce of Great Britain and France. At this period a great hatred of foreigners prevailed throughout the islands. The Shogun found himself compelled by the irresistible energy and power of civilization to make concessions, but these concessions were blamed by the people and used to his disadvantage. The position of foreigners residing in Japan was anything but agreeable: murders were frequent, and they literally lived with their lives in their hands. Still, foreign influence gradually extended, and the Shogun found himself threatened by the legations on the one hand and by his domestic enemies on the other. For some years of anarchy and disorder the contest continued, till in 1868 the chiefs of the four great southern clans obtained possession of the person of the Mikado—a boy of twelve, who had only recently ascended the throne—procured from him an edict abolishing the Shogunate, and defeated an able prince who had lately acceded to that office, who has since been permitted to reside as a private individual on his estate. Their next step was to remove the Emperor, as they now designate him, to Yeddo, and to carry on the administration in his name. The fall of the Shoguns, though probably hastened by the entrance of foreigners, might have happened under any circumstances; but a yet more extraordinary change remained to be effected. The Daimios have been humbled, and in many cases deposed, and are now pensioners on the lands they formerly owned, while their military retainers have been disbanded. This was rendered easier by the conduct of the Shoguns, who had forced the Daimios to reside most of the year in Yeddo. Like the French nobles whom Louis XIV. induced to frequent Versailles, they thus lost the affection of their dependents. The new Government has been principally composed of the retainers of the great clans, assisted by a few of the Court nobles of Kioto. They had risen to power by availing themselves of the popular hatred of foreigners; but they at once changed their course of action, and proceeded to imitate Western civilization. Europeans of all nations were engaged for the service of the Government, and young Japanese were sent forth on their travels and furnished with means to complete their education in Europe and America. They certainly must be remarkable men, as the changes they have effected are among the most wonderfully rapid which history records. A few years ago, if an Englishman rode outside of Yokohama, it was at the risk of being assassinated; now you may travel from one end of the country to the other without the smallest apprehension. Telegraphs extend all through the islands, and railways have been commenced. Numbers of small steamers frequent the inland sea and the rivers, and a great Japanese company runs from Yokohama to Shanghai. A government which in seven years has effected such a revolution deserves honour. We must not, however, be blind to the vast difficulties which await these remarkable men. The great mass of the Japanese people, like other Orientals, are probably ready to submit to any government which will enable them to pursue their avocations in security. If they have any political principle at all, it is veneration for the Divine person of the Mikado, and whoever makes use of that sacred name will probably secure their support. Whether they are prepared to make any sacrifices in his cause time only can show. But, with deposed Daimios and disbanded and disarmed samurai, there must be many floating elements of discontent. The Ministry has been raised to power by the great clans. Should these clans become unwilling or unable to support them, their authority will rest on a very precarious basis. Some soldier of fortune, who had the genius to attract to himself the disbanded two-sworded men, might plunge the country into a civil war. The Buddhist temples have been despoiled, and the Bonzes, or monks, expelled, but their dissatisfaction cannot but have a great influence on the people. The efforts of the Government to promote education deserve admiration; but in this, as in other of their improvements, they throw a great strain on their finances. It is impossible to open 53,000 schools, to construct a navy, to make railways, to erect light-houses, and to enter on other improvements without enormous expense, and the question arises, whether their revenue will be sufficient. As to their financial position, accounts differ, but the best-informed persons with whom I conversed represented the condition as bad. The land-tax supplies four-fifths of the revenue, so that a bad rice crop must be very serious to the exchequer. Should public credit break down, it may, as in other countries, prove the ruin of the administration.

It struck me as a grave mistake on the part of the Japanese to lavish large sums on their navy. They have nothing to fear from their immediate neighbours at sea, while it is impossible that they can resist the skill, courage, and experience of European seamen. This attempt to construct a navy seems a foolish imitation of the western powers, entailing great expense on the nation, and certain to prove a disastrous failure if called into action. As regards the army, the government have much greater justification for maintaining it on a large scale. The samurai, who have been disbanded by the Daimios, find themselves worse provided for and worse fed, owing to the change, and are besides unfitted by training and habits for the peaceful occupations of life. Hence they are probably less dangerous to the state in the regular army than left to roam through the country, and promote discontent. The Japanese think they must be prepared to resist any attack from the vast empire of China, and are jealous of the neighbouring peninsula of Corea. Then, too, in the case of a war with any of the great powers, though their troops would be no match for a European army, yet by taking advantage of their knowledge of the mountain ranges of their islands, they might occasion much trouble to a hostile commander. Still, though an army may be necessary to the Yeddo government, yet should it become dissatisfied, it may prove the cause of their overthrow. Such are some of the difficulties which await the present rulers of Japan. Except in their persecutions of the Native Christians their conduct has deserved admiration; and it is to be hoped that, avoiding the shoals and the quicksands with which their course is beset, they may place the throne of the Mikado on a firm basis. Should they fail in their efforts, should those beautiful islands become the scene of anarchy and civil war, the only solution would probably be an intervention on the part of one or more of the great powers.

The most important question in Japan, as in every other country, must be the religious. We have forced our way into the country, but if we only go there to trade, and do not impart to the people the blessings of Christianity, we shall have been a curse to them instead of a blessing. Japan was visited by the great missionary whose heroic virtues no difference of creed should make us ignore, St. Francis Xavier, in 1549, and the church which he founded continued in Japan till the massacre of Papenburg, in 1638. From that time the Jesuits were expelled, and except by the Dutch at Decima Christianity was unacknowledged. It is a remarkable fact that when French missionaries visited the country in 1858 they found communities of natives who, in spite of persecution and the absence of instruction, had maintained their Christian faith. In 1870 the Japanese government subjected these poor people to revolting and cruel persecution.[1] The representatives of the Treaty Powers remonstrated, but their representations were treated with cold civility, and passed unheeded. The Minister pleaded that "the Native Christians refused to join in the worship of the country. This is a direct act of rebellion against the Mikado, the Son of the Gods, and the chief of that religion which the Christians despise." On this ground all relief was refused. The administration appear to be themselves destitute of any religious belief, but they uphold Shintoism as a useful political engine. Their endeavours to suppress Buddhism, which is the faith of a large proportion of the people, cannot but produce discontent, and may, perhaps, lead to their downfall. The persecutions which they have authorized of the unfortunate Christians must deprive them of the sympathy which would otherwise be felt for their

[1] In the Soto Islands 400 Christians were arrested and many of them tortured, while the whole Christian population of Urakami, to the number of 3170 persons, was deported.

public services. I much regretted that I did not come in contact with any missionaries. Mr. Wylie, of Shanghai, who had lately visited Japan, told me that there are fifty Protestant missionaries labouring in the country, and that they are much encouraged in regard to their work. The Bishop of Victoria took a less hopeful view; but his lordship had not at the time I saw him visited the islands. Japan seems to me to have a peculiar and pressing claim on the Christian Church. In one sense missions are equally called for in every country. The Apostles were commanded "to go into all the world, and preach the Gospel to every creature;" and an immortal soul is equally valuable in the sight of our merciful God, whether it is the soul of a prince or a peasant, of a highly-educated and civilized man or of a savage. Still, particular mission-fields have special claims. India and our other possessions deserve the peculiar care of England, as we cannot doubt they have been confided to us by providence for the promotion of Christianity. In the case of Japan, the claim is that whereas in consequence of the entrance of foreigners, the country is in a transition state, there is a loud call to take advantage of the present conjuncture to send forth the messengers of the glad tidings of the Gospel of Peace. In other countries, humanly speaking, our children will be just as favourably or more favourably situated than we are for missionary labour. The neighbouring peninsula of Corea was at the time of my visit still closed to foreigners, even ships wrecked on the coast finding no succour, while some heroic Roman Catholic missionaries who entered the kingdom sacrificed their lives to the attempt. The Chinese still continue their resistance to western civilization; railways and telegraphs are unknown; travelling is discouraged; the interior of the empire is to a great extent unexplored; and the vast region apparently remains in the same condition which has prevailed for centuries past. But in Japan everything is in a state of change. The Japanese seem very anxious to imitate everything which comes from the west; and this disposition at least secures a consideration of the arguments in support of our holy religion. Surely this state of things is a loud call to the Church to be up and doing. Missionaries may now make their way in the country; and even should their labours be confined to the treaty ports, there is ample room for their utmost exertions. Intense interest attaches to the various problems involved in the present condition of Japan; but in spite of the rapid progress which has been made in material improvement and approximation to western ideas, the future looks to me a dark one. The one hope for the country is that God in His mercy should bless the preaching of the Gospel. Should this be the case all will be well. Otherwise I cannot but apprehend civil war, anarchy, and confusion.

CHAPTER III.

VOYAGE DOWN THE CHINESE COAST.

On the 24th we reached the Yellow Sea, so called from the colour it acquires from the great Chinese rivers which flow into it. After a cold, but otherwise pleasant voyage, we passed in the evening the North Saddle Lighthouse, marking the mouth of the Yangtsee Kiang. Next morning we reached the mouths of the Shanghai River, and were detained for some time waiting for the tide over the Woo Sung bar. This bar is a great impediment to the trade of Shanghai, but the Chinese will not allow it to be dredged, as they think it is a protection from invasion. The depth of water is said to be diminishing year by year, so that ere long the question will become a very serious one. At Woo Sung a number of Chinese war-junks were anchored. Of what use these unwieldly, though picturesque, vessels can be I could not ascertain. At length the tide rose, and we proceeded up the river, through a flat and desolate country, till we reached the magnificent city of Shanghai. Shanghai is an instance of what European energy can effect under the most unpromising circumstances. In the midst of a country as flat, as dull, and as uninteresting as can well be conceived, rises a city of palaces. Here, in spite of every disadvantage, has arisen the great emporium of trade in China. The river is thronged with the steamers of England, America, France, and other countries, while ashore you enjoy the comforts and the luxuries of civilization. The splendid mansions of the merchant princes and the shipping might make one fancy oneself in England if the Chinese costumes around did not undeceive one. I took up my quarters at the Central Hotel, which seemed comfortable, but, as owing to the hospitality of Mr. Boyce and Mr. Iveson, I never took a meal there, I saw but little of it. I called at the Consulate—a fine collection of buildings in the most conspicuous part of the English town—where I found that Mr. (about this time created Sir Thomas) Wade had just left on his return to Pekin. I much regretted not having the opportunity of making the acquaintance of this eminent public man, whose services to his country in the East it would be difficult to overrate. Before starting from home I had been warned by my friend and neighbour, Admiral Sir Charles Shadwell, who had just returned from the command of the China fleet, that I should be too late for Pekin, and this opinion was confirmed by Sir Harry Parkes. It was near the end of November, and Tientsin was expected shortly to be closed by ice. I might have got up to Pekin, but the difficulty would be how to get back, as, when the steamers cease to run, there is no means of returning except by a long, tedious, and difficult land journey. In Ceylon I met Mr. Eustace Smith, M.P., who had reached China a fortnight before me, and who told me he was warned by Sir Thomas Wade not to attempt the expedition. I had thought of going up the Yangtsee in one of the magnificent steamers which run to Hankow, and had applied for a passport for Nankin, when I consulted Mr. Boyce, an architect who has charge of the buildings of the British Government in China and Japan. He told me that the voyage to Hankow was too long for the time at my disposal, and recommended me to take the coasting steamers, which visit the ports of Foochow, Amoy, and Swatow. Mr. Iveson, a leading merchant here, was of the same opinion.

My friends were most kind in showing me Shanghai. On ascending the river the American concession first comes into view. It consists of a number of wharves for steamers along the water-side, with a street chiefly inhabited by Chinese, as the principal American merchants reside in the Bund in the English quarter. A small stream, called the Suchow Creek, separates the American from the English concession. On crossing the bridge the British Consulate is first reached, whence the Bund runs along the shore, where the principal business is conducted. Streets run off at right angles, where the Chinese traders reside. At the farther end of the Bund the French concession is reached. The government of the two towns shows the different characteristics of the nations to which they belong. Being concessions from the Chinese

Government, it is only natural that the consuls should exercise large powers, as they have to discharge judicial functions, and to see that the acts of the municipality do not contravene the stipulations of the Treaty of Tientsin. To such duties the English consul is limited, while the municipal government is confided to a council of seven members, annually elected by the residents, which discharges the functions of one of our corporations at home. The French consul, on the other hand, governs the concession. It is true there is a council, but this council is elected by the nominees of the consul, and, beyond giving advice, have little or no power. The buildings of the French quarter are very large, but it is a town nursed by the Government, not the result of spontaneous energy. Beyond the French concession is the Chinese city, surrounded by old, half-ruined walls, which, though useless against artillery, must be injurious to the health of the place. The streets are narrow and exceedingly dirty, a great contrast to those of Japanese towns, which are wide and clean. Mr. Boyce took me into several of the shops, in one of which they were making idols. The people are very polite in allowing you to walk through their shops without urging you to buy. On the 26th I called on Mr. Wylie, the agent of the British and Foreign Bible Society for these countries, who gave me a very interesting account of his work. He took me to see two opium-shops. At the first the proprietor told us that he had about 1000 visitors per diem, but was not doing as well as usual. They come in, some to take opium, which obliges them to lie down for the sake of inhaling it from their pipes, others only to smoke tobacco. Tobacco is supplied as an inducement to frequent the shop, in the hope that those, women as well as men, who begin to come there will ultimately become customers for opium. The appearance of these shops reminded me of that of a workman's *café* in Paris. There may not be so much to meet the eye as there is in an English gin-shop, as the effects of opium, though more speedily fatal to its victims, are less obvious to the passing observer. Hence I do not wonder that those who form their opinions from a cursory inspection of such shops as I visited should believe that their evils have been exaggerated. Against such I would place the testimony of those who live and labour among the Chinese. Mr. Wylie thinks opium-smoking is on the increase, and is demoralizing the population. Another friend of mine had been defending the trade, but on my asking if a house we were passing was an opium-shop, he casually replied, "No; an opium-house is like the lowest public-houses in England." I visited the General Hospital and the Gutzlaff Hospital, both very interesting institutions. Those in charge of them say that they are constantly applied to for medicine to cure people of the craving for opium, as, when the taste is once formed, it is most difficult to dispense with it. In fact, the craving for it is rarely, if ever, cured. Mr. Iveson took me into the Chinese quarter, to the office of a man who dealt in sycee silver. The mode of dealing here seems rather inconvenient. Calculations are for the most part made in taels instead of dollars. A tael is a weight of silver, and at the time of my visit was worth about $1⅓, though it is liable to fluctuations. The Europeans are in the habit of giving what they call chits, or small cheques, on the compradors of their houses. These chits are the substitutes of small money in other countries, and the residents here are saved the trouble of carrying money about with them. This is rendered necessary by the weighty character of Chinese money, which recalls to mind the iron of Lycurgus. In China, and also in Japan, a coolie is seen with an immense string of cash slung over his shoulder, as the only means of carrying it. The comprador is a Chinaman of superior position, who acts as cashier, and is attached to every mercantile establishment. He pays the chits presented to him, and is said generally to charge a liberal commission for himself. In fact, the poor coolie is entirely in his hands. Captain Painter was telling me a story illustrative of this. His ship, in coming up the river, had injured a Chinese junk, and, after some negotiation, the skipper agreed to take $50, which was thought to be less than the damage he had really suffered. Jardines gave him a cheque on their comprador, and Captain Painter accompanied him downstairs to the room of that worthy, who pretended to be busy, and told the master of the junk to wait until he was disengaged. The Captain divined that his object was to get rid of him, and make his own terms with the skipper, and, with kind feeling and sympathy for a brother sailor, resolved to thwart him.

This he did by telling him, "If you don't pay this cheque at once I shall go upstairs and complain." This brought the money without deduction.

The silk merchants' houses are curious. We visited one of them who was entertaining a large number of his connexions from the country. When a Chinaman comes to Shanghai to sell his silk he expects his broker to entertain him, who gets nothing in return but the commission on the sale. The evening was very cold, but the Chinese sat in an open court, keeping themselves warm by countless overcoats. Our friend said he had been anxious about the 1500 bales of silk he had, as they never insure, but he had now built a fire-proof warehouse, which made his mind easy about it. He was very hospitable, insisting on our taking tea. They make it by putting the tea into a cup, and then pouring boiling water upon it. The pigeon English spoken is curious. I should have thought it would have been as easy for the Chinese to learn a little good English as the execrable imitation of it which passes current in the treaty ports. Chinese is so difficult a language that merchants seldom attempt to learn it, and the knowledge of it is limited to missionaries and diplomatists. The different dialects are another great hindrance. Though the characters are the same, the inhabitants of neighbouring provinces cannot understand each other, and a gentleman told me that he had heard a Cantonese and a Swatow man unable to communicate in their own language talking pigeon English.

After dining with Mr. Boyce, I went on board the "Thales," Captain Painter, which did not, however, sail till next morning, the 27th. This was owing to the state of the tide on the Woo Sung bar. My host was going up the Yangtsee, but his steamer, though much larger and grander than the "Thales," was built for the river and not for the sea, and, drawing less water, got off earlier. Steamers are the universal mode of locomotion in China, and where they are unable to run travelling becomes difficult. The fares are high, that of the Peninsular and Oriental Company and the Messageries Maritimes being $80 from Shanghai to Hongkong. This, of course, I paid; but in my case it seemed very reasonable, as it involved a week's board in the steamers of Jardine, Matheson, and Co. to Foochow, and of Douglas, Lapraik, and Co. to Hongkong. In addition to their war-junks the Chinese are constructing an immense fort at Woo Sung to defend the entrance to the river. The navigation of the mouths of the Yangtsee is rendered difficult by immense banks of sand and mud, while the shores are very low. After leaving it the voyage lies through the Chusan archipelago, which recalls the

"Isles which crown the Ægean deep."

In beauty I think the Chinese Islands are superior to the Cyclades, but they have not the classical and historical associations which lend such a charm to Delos, and Melos, and Tenedos. The navigation of these islands is difficult, but Captain Painter was thoroughly acquainted with it. The North Saddle light is seen on the other bow from that on which it is visible coming from Nagasaki. Farther on a light-house is erected on the island of Gutzlaff, called, I presume, after the great Missionary of that name. On the 28th we continued our voyage through the islands. Immense numbers of fishing-boats were around us, and the poles attached to their nets reminded me of the seins used for pilchards in Cornwall. The inhabitants of these islands subsist for the most part by fishing. They grow a little rice, but exchange their fish for what they require on the mainland. Formerly they were much addicted to piracy, and are still ready to attack any ship in distress; but they find it useless to molest the large steamers which chiefly frequent these seas. After being delayed in the night by a fog, we reached, on the morning of the 29th, the mouth of the Ming River, where the scenery reminded me of the Italian Lakes. After a lovely sail we reached the Pagoda anchorage, so called from a Chinese Pagoda which stands on a promontory. Here we changed into a steam launch which took us to Foochow, where I was most hospitably received by Mr. Angus, of the great house of Jardine, Matheson, and Co. The Chinese merchants are distinguished by their hospitality. Except at Hong-kong and Shanghai, and there only recently, there are no hotels, and they entertain all travellers. After tiffin I took a stroll for two or three hours through the town, which is said to contain 500,000 inhabitants, including a floating population of 20,000. These people reside entirely in boats, bringing up their families on board. The husband is often engaged in the coasting-trade, and when they are absent the sampan, as the boat is called, is left in charge of the wife, who makes the children assist her in working it. Thus this strange population pass their lives, living and dying on the water. The usual mode of locomotion here is to be carried by coolies in chairs, but I preferred walking, as it gave me a good idea of a Chinese town. The different channels of the Ming are crossed by several bridges, and the streets are crowded by an enormous mass of human beings. To one lately arrived from England the scene is most striking and interesting. The town is dirty, but hardly so dirty as the native city of Shanghai. I met a large party of the gentlemen of Foochow at dinner, with whom I passed a very pleasant evening. They think the growth of opium is increasing in China, but that the Chinese will never dispense with Indian opium.

Next morning I took a sampan across the river to visit the monastery of Kushan. I was surprised to see a portrait of St. Francis in it, but on inquiry found the woman who owned it was a Roman Catholic. After going three or four miles down the river, and landing on the opposite side, we crossed some rice-fields and reached a temple. Hence a stone path frequently ascending long rows of steps, recalling by its resting-places, though it is not roofed over, the path from Bologna to the Church of the Madonna di S. Luca, leads up the mountain. It commands fine views of the valley of the Ming, with Foochow placed in the midst of the various channels of the river, of the mountains around, and, as you ascend higher, of the Pagoda anchorage and of the sea. The Monastery of Kushan is very extensive, consisting of a collection of gorgeous temples and buildings, with large figures of Buddha. Near it is a pond very full of sacred fish and a curious water-wheel. This Buddhist monastery recalls the great establishments of the Latin and Greek Churches, Monte Casino, Assisi, and that wonderful building which gives in the nineteenth century such a vivid picture of the abbeys of the middle ages, the great Monastery of St. Sergius at Troitsa, near Moscow. The scenery is very lovely, and I was told that by an excursion of two or three days farther up the Ming it becomes yet more beautiful. After lunching at the monastery and paying the fees to the chief priest, I returned down the mountain to the monastery at the foot, and reached Foochow by my sampan. Here I visited a curious temple near Messrs. Jardine's house, which is used as a sort of club by the Chinese. It was adorned with large numbers of flowers. I was shown a man smoking opium, who said he was fifty-eight, and had smoked it for twenty years, and whenever he was ill he took it and it cured him. He smoked four times a day. I find, whatever the views of Europeans on its effects, they discourage it among their employés, and some of them will not engage a man who uses it.

After taking leave of my kind hosts, I returned

with Captain Painter in the launch to the Pagoda anchorage, where I went on board the "Kwantung," Captain Pitman. The Pagoda anchorage, being the port of Foochow, is the residence of a colony of Europeans. The night was rough, and those who came on board late at night found some difficulty in embarking. Among these was Captain Grant, who had been for several years Commander of H.M. gun-boat "Midge," in which capacity he was much distinguished by his exertions against the Malay pirates. He was going home on being promoted to post-captain, and I had the pleasure of his company in my voyage to Galle. About 8 a.m., on the morning of December 1st, we weighed anchor. The Chinese are fortifying the mouth of the Ming, which is naturally very strong, though I am told their fortifications are worthless. We had a lovely sail down to the sea. These parts of China are very beautiful, as the gulfs up which the sea runs are fine and the mountains graceful. The hills are rather bare, and the vegetation is almost tropical, as the latitude of Foochow is 24°.30. There seem no facilities for travelling in the interior of China. Foreigners traverse the great rivers in steamers and natives in sampans. The roads are said to be very bad, and travellers have to be carried in chairs. The inns are very poor, and are not in the habit of accommodating strangers. Hence, though nothing is easier than to visit the ports of China, to explore the interior would be an undertaking of very great difficulty. What is easily seen of China is seen from the deck of a ship, and very few except missionaries have attempted to penetrate inland. After running out to sea we passed some islands called the White Dogs. From here to Cape Turnabout the ship rolled very much, as I was told is common in these seas. It was amusing to see sailors unable to stand, and to have to keep one's hand on one's glass at dinner, lest a lurch of the ship should upset it. Turnabout is said to be so named because ships beating up against the monsoon often had to turn round and return to Hongkong. After passing Turnabout we steered more West, and the ship became steadier. Early next morning we entered Amoy. The lovely sunrise, the graceful islands, the magnificent boulders of granite, and the surrounding mountains, made up a most striking panorama, and I never remembered to have beheld a more beautiful specimen of marine scenery.

The interior of Amoy, like that of other Chinese towns, is dirty. A population of 250,000 is claimed for it, but the returns of the rice consumed make 100,000 more probable. I was most kindly entertained by Mr. Pye, the leading merchant here, at his house on the beautiful island of Kulangsu, opposite to Amoy, over which it commands a view. He gave me a great deal of interesting information on the state of China, and as he speaks the language, and has travelled extensively, his knowledge is of great value. This information impressed me with the rotten condition of the Celestial Empire, and the changes which we may expect in this part of the world. He said the island of Formosa was well worthy of a visit, as the scenery is fine. I called on Mr. Dukes and Dr. Talmadge, missionaries here, who told me they have 2000 converts in Amoy, and an interesting work going on in the neighbouring country. They gave, on the whole, a satisfactory account of the native Churches, and spoke well of the moral character of the Chinese, of whom Dr. Talmadge has had twenty-nine years' experience. At five o'clock we left this charming place, which I conclude, however, must be fearfully hot in summer. Captain Pitman complained of his despatches coming so late on board, as the navigation out to sea is difficult. The night was rough, and rolling about in my berth prevented sleep. I was amused in the morning to find that sailors were inconvenienced in the same way as a landsman. About half-past seven in the morning we reached Swatow, and raced up the river, passing the "Yesso," another boat of the same company. Here, for the first time in my life, I entered the tropics, but the day was anything but tropical, as it was very cold. The poor lascars looked perished from it. I called on Dr. Gould and Mr. Gibson, missionaries labouring here, and met Dr. Kerr, another missionary of Canton. They spoke strongly of the difficulty of people giving up opium, though Dr. Kerr seemed to think the evil not as great as spirits. They seemed to believe in the large population commonly attributed to China, and gave a satisfactory account of the conduct of their native Christians. We talked about gambling, the great vice of the Chinese, and the infamous coolie trade from Macao, which has been recently stopped by the exertions of the English Government. They took me over their hospital and girls' school. I went on board the "Columbian," Captain Harvey, a P. and O. steamer, now being fitted out to take coolies to Singapore. A large number of Chinese go to the Straits. At lunch, on the "Kwantung," the conversation turned on the coolie trade. One of the captains present said that, twenty years before, he had been in the Chincha islands, and had seen the bodies of coolies who had been killed by the overseers thrown on board with the guano. He complained, however, that coolies sometimes came on board emigrant ships with a view to stirring up mutiny among their fellows. He said that Kworok-a-Sing, whose case came before the Judicial Committee of the Privy Council, was one of a class who took money five or six times to emigrate. This story sounds very improbable, as the man who knew the dangers and sufferings of an emigrant coolie ship would not willingly expose himself to them; but, be this as it may, Europeans who have been guilty of the fearful atrocities perpetrated in this accursed trade have no right to wonder if even the submissive Chinese is at last driven to resistance and to violence. We sailed, about four o'clock, through a difficult passage among the islands. The scenery was fine, though the evening was wet.

About eight o'clock on the morning of the 4th we reached Hongkong after a charming sail. Victoria, Hongkong, is one of the most beautiful cities

I have ever beheld. A magnificent land-locked harbour is surrounded by mountains, on the side of one of which the town rises, while the tropical trees lend a charm to the scene. At the time of my visit it looked like a paradise, but I am told that for the six or eight hot months it is one of the most disagreeable spots on earth. It is well lighted and paved, though the streets are very steep, and its appearance does much credit to the municipal authorities. The chair coolies climb the steep streets with wonderful celerity. I was most hospitably entertained by Mr. Kennard Davis, a son of the Rev. James Davis, of the Evangelical Alliance, and his companion, Mr. Leitch, at their house, which commands a lovely view over the harbour. I also received much kindness from the Governor, Sir Arthur Kennedy, the Chief Justice, Sir John Smale, the Bishop of Victoria, Admiral Ryder, Commodore Parish, and Dr. Eitel, of the London Missionary Society. The bishop was leaving, on the evening of my arrival, on a visitation of the coast ports, but I made a very interesting call upon him. He told me that, having been labouring for many years at Pekin, he found he now had to forget the Mandarin, and study the Cantonese dialect. The next day was Sunday, when I twice attended the cathedral, in the afternoon with Admiral Ryder, and dined in the evening with Sir Arthur and Miss Kennedy. The Governor strongly reprobated the coolie traffic, saying it was the worst form of slavery. He has put down the gambling-houses in Hongkong, and told me that when he originally came out Lord

Kimberly strongly urged him to do so at any cost. I recollect having been very much puzzled by a telegram on this subject in a blue book. General Whitfield, who succeeded as interim Governor during the absence of Sir R. MacDonnell, had suppressed gambling in the colony, upon which Lord Kimberley telegraphed to him not to interfere. When attention was called to the question in the House of Commons, the then Under Secretary for the Colonies, Mr. Knatchbull-Hugessen, palliated the gambling-houses, and pleaded that it would not be right to allow a Deputy-Governor to interfere with the policy of his predecessor. However, it would seem that, on reflection, the Colonial Office felt that they must not run counter to the general feeling of civilized mankind on this subject.

On Monday morning I started in the steamer "Flying Cloud" for Canton, which, under the influence of an opposition, accomplished the ninety miles in between six and seven hours. I was surprised to see the cabin filled with loaded muskets, and lascars with drawn swords walking the deck; but I was told that a steamer had been recently attacked by pirates, and the captain and many of the crew and passengers murdered. We at first sailed between rocky islands and the coast of the mainland, and then turned up the Canton river. The banks are flat, though hills are visible in the distance. The navigation must be difficult, as the river has several channels. At Whampoa is a bar, which large steamers cannot pass, while two pagodas near it look curious from the trees which grow from the galleries. In the days when all intercourse between China and Europe was carried on through Canton, Whampoa was a place of much importance. Proceeding a few miles further, Canton came in view. The city, with its walls, pagodas, some large forts, built for the protection of property, and a Roman Catholic cathedral, towering in the midst, looked very striking. The enormous number of junks and sampans, huddled together on the river, made the scene picturesque. The English live together on an island called Shamien, formed by the river on one side and a canal on the other, which is laid out like a park, and which presents a very pretty appearance. It has been conceded in the same way as the English town at Shanghai, and contains the houses of all the great merchants. Here I was most kindly entertained by Mr. Smith, of the firm of Thomas and Mercier. In the days when the whole of the tea-trade centered at Canton, foreigners were confined to a factory about the size of that of the Dutch at Decima. Shamien contains an English church, a club, and a concert-hall. The bridges which connect the island with the city have gates, which are guarded.

Next morning Mr. Piercy, of the Wesleyan Missionary Society, very kindly accompanied me about the town. Entering a sampan, we were rowed down the river to the other side of the city, through a succession of junks and sampans piled in endless rows. The junks have a bull's-eye painted near the prow, and the colour around indicates the town to which the boat belongs. Ningpo, for example, is black, Amoy green, and Swatow red. After landing we took chairs, each carried by three coolies, and proceeded through the narrow and dirty streets. The palace of the Viceroy is in Chinese style, with poor rooms and in bad repair. It was untenanted, as he had been recalled, and his successor had not arrived. The City Temple is large, while the corridor leading to the Temple of Horrors contains chambers where men are represented suffering the torments of hell. The Examination Hall is a large enclosure, containing 8650 small cells, one of which is assigned to each student when under examination. Similar halls are to be found in Pekin and several others of the large cities. The five-storied Pagoda and the Temple of Mercy are situated on a hill which commands an extensive and pleasing view over Canton and the surrounding country. The river flows through a wide and fertile plain, with graceful hills in the distance. Before the Temple is a tea-house, where we lunched. In a field below some troops were being drilled. The Chinese have the sense to maintain their national costume, much better fitted for a warm climate; and not, like the Turks, to ape Europeans by adopting the Western uniform. We visited a very fine pagoda, and took a walk on the walls, which are wide, and make a good promenade, which is apparently very little used by the natives. We called on Sir Brook Robertson, H.M. Consul, one of the greatest of Chinese scholars, and, from his long experience of the country, most conversant with China and the Chinese. He palliated the use of opium, but said he thought the increased production in China threatened the Indian revenue. People prefer Havanna cigars, but Manillas are so much cheaper in the East that they are almost exclusively used. In like manner China opium, though not so well liked, will ere long, on account of its cheapness, drive Indian out of the market. He believes in the large population commonly assigned to China. His opinion on this point is equal, if not superior, to that of any other man; but, considering that the population of some of the towns with which we are best acquainted proves to be less than it was believed to be some years ago, it would seem as though that of the empire at large may have been overrated. He says the coolie trade has been entirely suppressed, and thinks Canton only fourth in size among the cities of China. We visited some opium-shops, where some of those we saw looked victims to it, while others appeared not to have suffered. One man we talked to admitted to spending *5d.* a day—half his earnings—in smoking. These shops were not well fitted up, like those I saw at Shanghai, but wretched, dirty, and mean. Mr. Piercy introduced me and interpreted for me to the secretary of a native society for the suppression of opium-smoking, whose object is to diminish the vice by moral suasion. After dining with Mr. and Mrs. Piercy, I met at the house of Mr. Chalmers, of the London Missionary Society, about twelve gentlemen interested in the opium question. The statements made of the evils were very affecting. Mr. Nye, an American merchant, said he had come to Canton in 1833, and of the ten great Hong merchants who at that time were the channel of communication between European and Chinese traders, and who were possessed of great wealth, the families of nine had been brought to ruin by opium-smoking. When the head of the family died, his sons took to opium, neglected their business, and at last became bankrupt. A town was mentioned between Amoy and Foochow which was being depopulated by the prevalence of the vice. Young men are drawn into the habit, and become ruined by it. It is becoming very common among literary men, and the opium-pipe is often offered in private houses among the Chinese. It is not, as far as I could gather, tendered to Europeans; but Mr. Morton, my fellow-passenger in the "Alaska," when I afterwards met him at Bombay, told me he had been shown over several of their houses by wealthy Chinese, and in most cases he was taken into the opium-smoking room. The missionaries are strict in enforcing the rule that no opium-smoker is admitted as a member of their Churches, and expressed their opinion that, unless active measures are taken to stop the evil, China will be ruined by this vice. They said that in proclaiming the Gospel three reproaches on Europeans used to be thrown in their teeth—opium, the coolie trade, and the gambling-houses licensed by the British Government at Hongkong. The two last causes of reproach have been stopped, but the first becomes worse year by year. Opium is still produced by the British Government in India, is still carried in British ships to China, and is still sold by British subjects to the unfortunate Chinese. Is it wonderful that heathen should fail to be impressed with the excellence of a religion whose professors inflict on them such evils? The account which these excellent and devoted men gave of their labours was interesting. They seem to be able to go freely about among the Chinese, and are able to preach in public places, even in the porticos of temples. The fact that the Roman Catholics have been allowed to build a large cathedral shows the way to be open for missionary labour. The Church of Rome has been very active in her missions in China, and it becomes Protestants to be the same. Those who go forth in the service of the Gospel demand all the sympathy which we can give them. They have to live far from their friends and their native land, in a climate which, though pleasant in winter, must be most trying in summer, and to submit to the dangers to which such an exile exposes them. Their reward is hereafter, but they deserve the support and the prayers of the Church at home.

On the 8th I returned to Hongkong, my kind host, Mr. Smith, coming down in the same boat. On these steamers one sees a good deal of opium-smoking, the Chinese bringing their pipes on board, lying down, lighting them at the little lamps which are essential to the process, inhaling the smoke, and then becoming stupefied or going to sleep. It is a curious circumstance that no Chinaman, however rich, likes to travel in the first cabin of a steamer. You constantly meet Japanese gentlemen, but rarely or never Chinese. The wealthy Chinese, with his servant to attend upon him, prefers remaining among his countrymen. I regretted that time did not permit me to visit Macao, the Portuguese colony which forty years ago was the sole European settlement in these seas. It has latterly obtained an infamous notoriety as the starting-port of vessels engaged in the coolie traffic. Now that this traffic has been suppressed, I was told that the town is in a very declining condition. The barracoons were the great sight of the place, and they are now closed. We accomplished our voyage in six hours, and I reached Victoria in time to pay some calls. The first was on the excellent Chief Justice, Sir John Smale, a man to whom humanity is deeply indebted for his successful exertions to suppress the infamous coolie trade. The noble stand which he made on this question entailed at the time a great sacrifice, as the officials of Hongkong were hostile to him, and the society of the colony generally opposed to him till his labours were crowned with success. I did not find him at home, but he most kindly came on board the "Golconda" to see me off next day. I saw Dr. Eitel, of the London Missionary Society, who took me to a Chinese wedding. The bride, the daughter of the printer to the Mission, sat in a thick veil receiving visitors, who made her presents, and giving them tea. The bridegroom was a Chinese preacher. I dined with Commodore Parish, on board the "Victor Emanuel." Hongkong is the headquarters of the Chinese fleet, and, as the Admiral has to cruise from the Straits to Japan, the Commodore is often in command here. During the summer this must be a very unpleasant station, as the heat is intense. In consequence of our large commerce in these seas, we are compelled to keep a strong fleet, and from the difficulties of communication a large discretion has to be confided, not only to the Admiral, but to the various commanders of the ships. The Admirals of some other fleets may be of higher rank, but from the delicate nature of our relations with the Celestial Empire, from the long distance from home, and from the imperfect state of telegraphic communication, the Commander-in-Chief of the Chinese squadron has duties to discharge of a more responsible nature than probably any other officer afloat.

The 9th was my last day in China. Early in the morning I started with Mr. Davis to walk up to the Peak. Passing the public gardens, which are remarkable for their tropical plants and beautifully laid out, we ascended a wild gorge, and, passing several pretty villas, reached the Peak—a hill which rises to the height of 1800 feet, and commands a view over the island, the town, the harbour, and the adjacent mainland. The calm sea, the port crowded with ships bearing the flags of all nations, the town lying below in the midst of tropical vegetation, and the barren mountains, rocks, and islands around, form a striking scene. Dr. Eitel took me to see an opium-boiling establishment, where opium is boiled preparatory for use, much of it to be sent to California, for consumption there. This and other houses are licensed by a man who farms the right to boil opium, and pays the Colonial Government 120,000 dollars (24,000*l.*) a year, for three years, for the privilege. There were eighteen men at work, preparing it to be put in boxes and sent to California. I was informed that Dr. Dudgeon had recently visited this establishment, and questioned the proprietor, who said he considered opium a great evil, and would not keep a man in his employment who smoked it, but he carried on the business for the sake of profit. Dr. Eitel says it is destroying the population, as opium-smokers have no children.

I now prepared to leave Hongkong. Business here is carried on in dollars, and one does not hear of taels as at Shanghai. The Oriental and other banks issue notes, which are a great convenience. Sir John Smale, Dr. Eitel, and Mr. Davis, most kindly accompanied me on board the P. and O. steamer "Golconda," Captain Anderson, and saw me off. At twelve the ship started, but owing to a difficulty in getting round in the harbour it was one before we got away. At sunset we were losing sight of the Chinese islands, the last of which, like the last rock of Japan, is called the Asses' Ears. I could have wished my time in China had been longer, but, being prevented from visiting Pekin, it seemed better to devote to India time which to every traveller who does not wish to be caught by the hot season must be necessarily limited. Under any circumstance, travelling beyond the Treaty Ports is not easy to those who have no knowledge of the language, as, owing to the difference of dialects, interpreters are not readily procured. Hence all that one can see must be seen from the deck of a ship. The present is pre-eminently an age of change. Hardly any important country can be pointed out in which great alterations have not occurred in our own time. China, of all countries, attempts a determined hostility to change. Railways and telegraphs have created a revolution in the civilized world, and are extending their influence over semi-barbarous nations. Even the Ottoman Empire is traversed by telegraphs, and permits railways. China alone offers a determined opposition to their introduction. Their excuse as regards railroads is, that their construction might desecrate the graves of their ancestors, whom they worship; but they cannot avail themselves of this plea in regard to telegraphs. The hostility evidently arises from a settled determination to resist all intercourse with foreigners. Little seems known of the intrigues of the Imperial Palace, though rumour says that the late Emperor was murdered by the Dowager Empress, a most vicious woman, who, nevertheless, must possess great talent for intrigue, as she has managed to retain power for a long course of years. An infant Emperor, with two Dowager Empresses, while Prince Kung, the only able man of the family, is not consulted, must of necessity form a wretched Government, and it is no wonder that the Mandarins are able to oppress the provinces which they rule.[1] The Taeping

[1] It is only fair to admit that in Li-Hung-Chang, the pre-

rebellion must have caused immense suffering to the nation, though, had it succeeded, it might have founded a different and a better Government. These Oriental nations, with no ability for self-government, must depend for their happiness on the character of their rulers, and the present dynasty appears to be effete and tottering to its fall. It may be upset by some soldier of fortune, who has the genius to seize the Empire; or it may fall a prey to some great Western Power. When I hear people frightening themselves about the advance of Russia towards India, I think that a more tempting game presents itself for Muscovite ambition in China. The two empires are contiguous, and the Colossus of the North would not have to contend with a civilized nation to conquer these teeming millions of unwarlike Asiatics. The Chinese, when drilled by European officers, are said to make soldiers, but of course their army could not contend with that of any of the Great Powers. The central authority seems to be very weak, and unable to maintain its authority in the provinces. At the time of my visit, the mission to Yunan to inquire into the murder of Mr. Margery had just started, and many feared that our envoys ran great risk. The Government, finding itself too weak to interfere in Formosa, was obliged to allow the Japanese to take their own course. I found

sent Grand Secretary of the empire, and Governor of Chihli, China possesses a ruler of the first ability, and one, moreover, who, if report may be trusted, is not likely to commit himself to a policy of blind resistance to change.

many people, especially among the merchants, blaming Sir Thomas Wade for want of firmness with the Court of Pekin, and crying out for a spirited, in other words a warlike, policy. To such persons I remarked, "What is it that you propose to do? In the first place, Sir T. Wade only carries out—very ably, it is true—the instructions he receives from Downing Street. But suppose Lord Derby was to take a different line. We have had two or three small wars with China. If we have another, it must be a war on a very different scale, and we must exact material concessions at the conclusion of it. The least we can ask is the sovereignty of the island of Formosa, and of the country round Shanghai, including the mouths of the Yangtsee. If we carried on such a war, and took this territory, we should probably overthrow the present dynasty, and plunge the country into anarchy. Having once begun, we should be driven in China, as we have been in India, to enlarge our dominions, whether we wished it or not, and finally we should be obliged to govern China as we govern India. Are you prepared for such a course? If you are not, it is a matter of necessity that England should pursue a policy of great forbearance." Those of whom I asked these questions were obliged to admit that they could not contemplate such a contingency, and I told them that I believed no English Minister, least of all Lord Derby, would pursue such a policy. No doubt the difficulties which we have to encounter in dealing with Chinese diplomacy are great, but it is important that we should not allow such difficulties unduly to influence us, but should pursue a course of moderation and justice. The mercantile community are undoubtedly greatly influenced by the depression of trade which has prevailed for some years. When men go to the other side of the world to make their fortunes, it is naturally very discouraging to find some of those fluctuations, to which all business is liable, prevailing, and to be obliged to remain abroad for a much longer period than they had intended. This feeling is aggravated by the recollections of the large fortunes which in former days have been made in the China trade. Hence it is no cause for surprise if people, under such circumstances, think that the Government might do much to remedy the existing state of things. It is no wonder if they cannot enter into the views of a minister who has the responsibility of advising her Majesty in the exercise of what the late Lord Derby most truly called "that most awful prerogative of the Crown, the declaring of war," or of the British people, who have to pay the taxes which it would occasion. The course pursued by England cannot but be an obstacle to Christian missions. To the Chinese we must appear as a nation who force on them a poisonous and pernicious drug, who have carried on unjust wars for the protection of our trade, and who, in former days, encouraged gambling in our dependency, while another European nation supported the infamous coolie emigration. Such charges against Christian countries must prove a great impediment to the success of the Gospel when preached by the missionaries. These holy and devoted men are subjected to many privations. They have to reside far from their friends and native land, in an unhealthy climate, and, after acquiring a difficult language, to labour among a heathen population. Nevertheless, servants of God—both from Europe and America—go forth in the service of their Master, and, in spite of all discouragements, they have the reward of seeing that His blessing attends their labours. Nor should any difference of opinion prevent our doing justice to the heroism displayed by the Roman Catholics. For centuries the Roman Catholics, and especially the Jesuits, have laboured in China, and have penetrated further than any other foreigners. The celibacy enforced by the Latin Church has been productive of many evils, and in a distant exile it seems peculiarly important that a minister should have the consolations of domestic life; nevertheless, it must be admitted that the absence of every tie to life may be an assistance in undertaking perilous expeditions into remote and barbarous regions, and may enable the missionary more easily to obtain a footing among the people. Great complaints have been raised against the missionaries, both Protestant and Roman Catholic, and it has been alleged that they are the great hindrance to peaceful intercourse with China. No doubt the Imperial Government is opposed to all attempts at proselytism, and would rather see the missionaries expelled; but for Christians who believe that our great end in our intercourse with heathen nations should be the spread of the Gospel, this consideration has no weight. It is our duty, nationally and individually, to do all that lies in our power to uphold the hands of our brethren who are taking the glorious message of "peace on earth, and good-will towards men" to a benighted people. But it may, with great reason, be denied that the missionary question has much, if anything, to do with our difficulties with China. These difficulties arise from conduct unworthy of our Christian profession, which has disgusted both the Government and the people of China.

There are three questions connected with China, in which, when I was in Parliament, I took some interest—the opium trade, Hongkong gambling, and the coolie trade. We often hear it said that it is hypocrisy to object to opium when we ourselves derive so large a revenue from alcohol. Every one must deplore the fearful evils produced by drunkenness in our own country, but it may be pointed out that the two questions are not similar. The use of wine dates from the earliest periods which history records, and in many nations it has been used with little or no abuse. Moreover, alcohol, in one form or other, is constantly prescribed by physicians to their patients, and most of us consider its use important to our health. So far as the action of the English Government is concerned, it has simply been by heavy taxation and by restrictions in the sale to discourage consumption. Opium, on the other hand, is only used medically in cases of severe illness; smoking it is not prescribed by physicians; and without asserting that it is never used in moderation, it has a fearful tendency to enslave its victims. Moreover, the action of the Indian Government has not been to discourage production, but to regulate it with a view to the largest possible revenue. It is an Indian rather than a Chinese question, and for the present I must merely allude to the results in regard to China. A great authority, with whom I conversed on the subject, pleaded that the taste for opium did not originate with its introduction by the East India Company, but must have existed in China long before we traded there, as we then knew nothing, and now know little, of the interior provinces. For the honour of England, I hope this view may be true, as it would be a comfort to think that, though we have undoubtedly encouraged, we did not introduce this vice; but I can but fear there is no evidence in support of the theory. Opium is now so general that people cannot conceive that a century since it was unknown. My friend believed that the growth in China is large and increasing, and has existed for a long course of years. This seems the general view, and I can but fear that the evil has grown to such an extent that it is no longer in our power to put a stop to it. In former days the Chinese Government was sincerely desirous to suppress the consumption, and proved their earnestness by their refusal to legalize the trade by a customs' duty, and by the sacrifices they made at the time of "the opium war" of 1839, of which Mr. Gladstone said, "A war more unjust in its origin, a war more calculated to cover this country with permanent disgrace, I do not know and I have not read of." Though beaten in this war, the Emperor of China refused to derive a revenue from the demoralization of his people by legalizing the trade. Now, defeated in subsequent wars, and weakened by internal dissensions, the Imperial Government may not have the power, if it has the will, to forbid the importation and the cultivation of opium. It is a sad chapter in our national history. The very nation which has been foremost in suppressing the slave-trade, and which paid 20,000,000*l*. to abolish slavery, has, for the sake of illicit gain, demoralized an unoffending people. I could fill a volume with quotations from eminent men, denouncing the trade. I shall content myself with one testimony, that of Baron Von Hubner,[2] the greatest European statesman who has travelled in the East, who, after bearing witness to the upright and honourable conduct of the merchants on all occasions, adds, "There is, of course, one dark side—the opium trade—now perfectly legal, but immoral in my eyes, from the fact that it furnishes a poison to the people, the deleterious effects of which, as far as I myself have seen, cannot possibly be exaggerated. Those who are most interested in this trade do not attempt to deny it." Similar evidence might be quoted to any extent. I give full credit to Indian statesmen (to whose difficulties in connexion with this subject I shall hereafter have to allude) and to China

[2] He was Austrian Ambassador at Paris in 1859, and it was to him that Napoleon addressed the celebrated declaration which preceded the war.

merchants, for believing that the evils of opium have been greatly exaggerated; but, after making every allowance, I cannot but think that the British people have been culpable in regard to this question.

I have already had occasion to say something in regard to the gambling-houses at Hongkong. It seems not to be doubted that gambling is a great and an inherent vice of the Chinese. All that the British Government can do is to discourage it. The policy of Sir Richard Macdonnell to license houses for the purpose, for the sake of a revenue of 180,000 dollars (35,000*l.*) per annum, was obviously immoral. When all the Great Powers of the world prohibit establishments of this description, it would have been impossible for English Ministers to permit their continuance in a Crown Colony, and it is only justice to Lord Kimberley and to Mr. Knatchbull-Hugessen to say that, as soon as attention was called to the matter, they took immediate steps to suppress them. We may now rejoice to believe that England is clear from all complicity with a vice which was formerly openly permitted in the colony.

These gambling-houses were the means of supporting a trade which was a curse to China. When a coolie had lost his last cent. he would stake his liberty on a final throw of the dice, and if it went against him he would hand himself over to those who recruited coolies for Cuba or Peru.[3] They placed him on board

[3] I quote from statements made in Parliament, February 16th, 1872, the correctness of which was admitted by Lord Enfield, the Under-Secretary for Foreign Affairs.

a steamer, carried him to Macao, confined him in the barracoons, and shipped him off for his destination The horrors of the voyage it would be difficult to exaggerate. A crowded ship has discomforts under the most favourable circumstances, but these unfortunate emigrants were packed together as closely as possible; and when the owners and captains of the ships were actuated simply by the desire to make as much money as possible out of their human cargo, no wonder if the sufferings were horrible. The Chinese coolie traffic vied with the African slave-trade in its abominations. Men were decoyed from their homes, made to sign agreements in a language which they did not understand, forced on shipboard, and sent to a distant land never to return. It would be a horrible lot for any man, and for a Chinaman, with his intense desire to lay his bones in his native land, it has additional horrors. Attention was called to the trade in 1871, by the case of the "Dolores Ugarte," a vessel which sailed from Macao for Peru, on May 15th, with a cargo of 656 coolies. On the 17th, a fire having broken out, the hatchways were fastened down, the crew took to the boats, and 600 Chinese were left to their fate. A few of them managed to escape, and their evidence showed that they had been induced by acquaintances, on pretence of work, to make the journey to Macao; that, instead of having their expectations realized, they were cruelly treated, and threatened by emigration agents; that they signed papers which were neither explained nor read to them, and that they were carried on board ship against their will. Such was the history of the unhappy men left to perish in the "Dolores Ugarte." On a previous voyage of the same ship eighteen coolies jumped overboard in consequence of ill-treatment, twenty-five died from want, and forty-three were in such a hopeless state of disease that they were landed at Honolulu. Such were the horrors of the voyage, but the fate of those who reached their destination was equally miserable. The Chincha Islands are perfectly destitute of vegetation, and the Chinese who are decoyed there for the term of three years seldom live to complete their slavery. They are detained by an armed force, huddled together in the most miserable manner, fed only after performing a certain amount of labour, and subjected to horrible tortures. They are hung by ropes round the waist from sunrise to sunset, without food during that period, for one, two, or more days. No wonder that the poor creatures often cut short their sufferings by suicide. Those who were sent to the mainland fared little better, as a large Peruvian farmer would purchase three or four hundred, lock them up at six at night in an enclosure, turn them out at half-past four in the morning under armed and mounted drovers, and give them only two meals a day of rice or beans. Those who live out their contract are afraid to ask their liberty lest they should be flogged. Such was the wretched fate of coolie emigrants to Peru.

The Committee of the Aborigines Protection Society, in a memorial addressed to Lord Salisbury on Sept. 2,

1874, quote the following extract from a despatch which Mr. Thomas, the American Minister at Lima, had addressed to the Secretary of State at Washington in April of the preceding year :—"Having made careful inquiry on the subject, I am prepared to say that the treatment of these unfortunate Chinese, thus forced violently from their homes by the landlords of Peru, by whom crowds of them are employed, is more harsh than that to which slaves in the United States were formerly subjected."

As regards Cuba, we have the evidence of Commissioners appointed by the Chinese Government to inquire into the condition of Chinese coolies in that island. These gentlemen, one Chinese, one Englishman, and one American, Messrs. Ch-en-Tampin, Macpherson, and Huber, have made an elaborate report dated October 20th, 1874. They say, "All investigations of Chinese were conducted verbally and in person by ourselves. The depositions and petitions show that eight-tenths of the entire number declared that they had been kidnapped or decoyed; that the mortality during the voyage from wounds caused by blows, suicide, and sickness, proves to have exceeded ten per cent.; that, on arrival at Havanna, they were sold into slavery, a small proportion being disposed of to families and shops, while the large majority became the property of sugar-planters; that the cruelty displayed towards those of the former class is great, and that it assumes, in the case of those of the latter, proportions that are unendurable. The labour, too, on the plantations is shown to be excessively severe, and the food to be insufficient. The hours of labour are too long, and the chastisements by rods, whips, chains, &c., productive of suffering and injury. During the past years a large number have been killed by blows, have died from the effects of wounds, and have hanged themselves; cut their throats, poisoned themselves with opium, and thrown themselves into wells and sugar-caldrons. It was also possible to verify, by personal inspection, wounds inflicted upon them, the fractured and maimed limbs, blindness, the heads full of sores, the teeth struck out, the ears mutilated, and the skin and flesh lacerated, proofs of cruelty patent to all." Such is the report of the Commissioners; and as a samplo of the evidence on which that report is founded, the following statements made by coolies, taken at random from hundreds of others, may be quoted. Lim-show and four others state, "We were decoyed to the Macao barracoons, and, though not inspected by any Portuguese officials, were forced by soldiers to embark, while no one heeded the cries for aid which we uttered on the way." A petition from nearly 100 native districts complains that "Spanish vessels come to China, and, suborning the visions of our countrymen, by their aid carry away full cargoes of men, of whom eight or nine out of every ten are decoyed." Ch'en Yu-shu and four others say, "Whether we are disposed of as domestic slaves, or sold to sugar warehouses or shops, we are dealt with as dogs, horses, or oxen, badly fed, and deprived of rest, so that a single day becomes a year."

Wang Chang deposes, "I found the chaining and flogging so unendurable during the first six months of my service that I attempted suicide." Hung Feng-chi and eleven others state, "We had to endure every kind of suffering. When our terms of service were drawing to their close, we thought that we could rely upon our contracts, and that we should be able to go out and reap advantage; but these documents were held as invalid, and our freedom was withheld." Ho A-pu deposes, "If we went outside only a few steps we were regarded as attempting to escape, and were seized. Thus no one dared to prefer complaints." Wang Mu-Chow says, "Finding the labour too arduous, I made a complaint to the officials, and the latter recommended my master to be less exacting, and to supply me with sufficient food. He assented; but, when he had brought me back, he forced me to work with chained feet during seven months." Chu Afu "saw a native so severely beaten that he drowned himself. Besides, there were seven other men who committed suicide." Such are a few of the statements which justify the Commissioners in the conclusions at which they have arrived; and I think it must be admitted that nothing more horrible ever found place in an official document. Truly, "the dark places of the earth are full of the habitations of cruelty." The Chinaman, like the native of other countries, has his faults; but, properly treated, he is an industrious labourer, well calculated to promote the development of the land where he settles. That he should be subjected to this terrible slavery is a disgrace to the civilization of the 19th century. To Lord Granville belongs the honour of having stopped this abominable traffic. His remonstrances with the Portuguese Government were at last crowned with success, and he had the satisfaction, before he left office, of seeing the barracoons closed at Macao. The report of the Commissioners, from which I have quoted, has induced the Chinese Government to prohibit immigration to Cuba; and therefore, so far as China is concerned, we have no longer to deplore the horrors of a trade as bad, or worse, than the slave-trade. Still, numbers of unhappy Chinese are still pining, in violation of right and justice, on the plantations of Cuba, and it must be the duty of that illustrious statesman, who now guides the Foreign policy of England, to remonstrate on the subject.

It is a lamentable consideration that, when we had fondly hoped the slave-trade had been abolished in the days of our fathers, we should find it in our own time in as fearful activity as ever. We have stopped the accursed traffic on the West Coast of Africa; but on the East Coast, on the India seas, and on the Pacific Ocean, we have witnessed atrocities such as those which roused the righteous indignation of Clarkson and Wilberforce. We have had occasion to employ the burning words of the poet Cowper, written a century ago,—

> "But ah! what wish can prosper or what prayer,
> For merchants rich in cargoes of despair,

Who drive a loathsome traffic, gauge and span,
And buy the muscles and the bones of man?
The tender ties of father, husband, friend,
All bonds of nature in that moment end;
And each endures, while yet he draws his breath,
A stroke as fatal as the scythe of death."

England has made many sacrifices for the suppression of the slave-trade, and for the abolition of slavery; but the time has not yet arrived when her efforts can be permitted to terminate.

CHAPTER IV.

THE STRAITS SETTLEMENTS AND CEYLON.

There are two principal lines of steamers running to China—the Peninsular and Oriental, commonly called the P. and O., sailing from Southampton and Venice, and the Messageries Maritimes, which run to Marseilles. There are, besides, several mercantile lines, which take passengers at cheaper rates with inferior accommodation. The English and French boats leave China alternate weeks. The English mercantile community in China prefer the Messageries, alleging, as a reason, that they are taken to Marseilles without change of vessel. They have the advantage of being cheaper, as they give beer and wine, which are charged for on the P. and O.; but for my part, if it comes on to blow, I prefer being under the care of an English captain.

The "Golconda" was the first of five P. and O. vessels in which I sailed between Hongkong and Brindisi, and in all of them I received much kindness from the captains and officers. It is much to be regretted that the Company have thought it necessary to reduce the salaries of their employés. No doubt their profits have fallen off, and the fact of their rivals, the Messageries, being supported by the French Government with an enormous subvention as a school for their seamen, places them at a disadvantage; but it is never good policy to deal stingily with old servants, and the tendency of the reduction must be to lower the high position which has been maintained by the officers in their service. The fare from Hongkong to Brindisi is 85*l.*, with leave to stop in India. Not being aware of this, I only booked to Calcutta, and again from Bombay; but on my return to England the Company very liberally repaid me the difference.

We made 246 knots on December 10th, 272 on the 11th, 283 on the 12th, 303 on the 13th, and 270 on the 14th, leaving 83 to Singapore. This was a very fast run for one of these boats, which are timed at about ten knots per hour; but we had a tremendous monsoon in our favour. It was much such weather as the "Alaska" encountered, only now we were running before a fresh gale. On one occasion the log was hauled fourteen knots, when Captain Grant exclaimed, "This is the first time in my life that I have ever gone fourteen knots." I told him it was evident he had never crossed the Atlantic in a mail steamer. Our course was only a little to the west of south, and it got hotter hour by hour. For four days, except one or two small islands, we were out of sight of land. They say it is unusual to take the monsoon so near to the Equator. It was full moon, which reminded me of Byron's description of—

> "The lovely light
> Which but becomes an Eastern night."

The 14th was very hot, the thermometer being 80°, while it constantly rained, and at times poured. The heat and damp of the Equator one would think must be very trying; but the residents seem to enjoy better health than one might expect. Captain Anderson, not caring to reach Singapore a day before his time, took down sail and slowed his engines, which he had previously been unable to do. About half-past nine we reached the roads of Singapore, and anchored for the night. The lights of the town looked well from the water. On being boarded from H.M.S. "Egeria," we learnt that there had been a skirmish between some men of the 10th regiment and the Malays, in which, after two Englishmen had been killed, and two mortally wounded, three stockades of the Malays were taken. When at Kobe I heard a very exaggerated report of disturbances at Singapore, it being even stated that all the Europeans in the colony had been murdered. This was the extent to which the murder of the resident, Mr. Birch, was exaggerated by report—

> "Fama qua non malum aliud velocius ullum
> Mobilitate viget viresque acquirit eundo."

At Shanghai there were rumours that Admiral Ryder had taken the fleet to the Straits; but it turned out not to be the admiral but General Colbourne, who took down a detachment of troops from Hongkong, and was joined by the Buffs from India. On approaching Singapore, the city of Johore lies to the north. The enlightened administration of the Maharajah of Johore deserves the admiration with which it is regarded by the European community of the Straits. His Highness had at this time gone to Calcutta to attend the Prince's Durbar.

Early in the morning of the 15th the "Golconda" moved into the Inner Harbour, where the P. and O. boats lie. Captain Anderson was anxious to leave the same day, but the Post Office would not allow him to do so, as the Company are under contract to remain twenty-four hours here. This I was very glad of, as I was hospitably entertained by Mr. Donaldson, a lawyer here, whose wife is a daughter of my friend and late colleague, Mr. Eastwick. The roads run through tropical vegetation, palms, bananas, bamboos, &c. Singapore is an imposing city. The cathedral and public buildings are fine, and the gorgeous costumes of the Malays and Indians render it more picturesque than a Chinese town. There is a large foreign population from all parts of the East, but chiefly from China and Madras. I visited the Courts, where the number of languages spoken entails numerous interpreters. Punkas are necessary everywhere, on shipboard, at business, and at meals. The thermometer was only 74° to 76°, as low as it ever is, though they say it rarely exceeds 86°. It rains almost daily, though I was told the twenty-four hours' steady rain I experienced is not common. The sun being vertical at the equinoxes (the latitude is only 1° 14′ N.), and the Java wind blowing in July, make the climate very oppressive most of the year. The heat, the luxuriant vegetation, and the constant rain, would seem likely to produce malaria; but the place appears wonderfully healthy. The damp, however, seems to affect horses, who do not get through the work here they do in India. Next morning Mr. Donaldson took me to breakfast with the Hon Mr. Whampoa, a great Chinese merchant, and a member of the Legislative Council, where we met Captain Grant and Captain Parlby, of the Royal Artillery, who was our fellow-passenger on the "Golconda" from Hongkong to Ceylon. Mr. Whampoa's house, which is full of Chinese and Japanese curiosities, and his gardens, which contain the finest tropical plants, are the great sight of Singapore. Though dressing in national costume, and eating little himself, he gave us a European meal. He is much respected in the colony, and I have been very glad to see, since my return, that the Queen has conferred on him the Companionship of St. Michael and St. George. I have often regretted that successive administrations have not been more liberal in recommending her Majesty to confer honours on distinguished colonists, as I believe it would do much to bind the Empire together. The day cleared up, and the country looked beautiful, when, after taking leave of my kind host and hostess, I returned on board the

"Golconda," which sailed at 4 p.m. It was at Singapore I heard of the purchase of the Suez Canal shares, which seemed to give great satisfaction to the English community here, as in other parts of the East.

From Singapore to Penang is a voyage of two nights and one day. On the right are the Malay hills, where fighting was then going on. Captain Grant was very familiar with the district, as he had two years before conducted some successful operations against the Malay pirates. On the left is the low-lying land of Sumatra. About half-past eight on the morning of the 18th we reached Penang. The wooded hills at the back of the town make the scene very beautiful. In company with Mr. Williams, the doctor of the ship, I made an attempt to visit a waterfall. Driving for about two miles through beautiful groves of cocoa-nut and bamboo, we left our "gindy," as they call the small carriage of the country, and turned up a hill. Having mistaken the path, we had a steaming-hot walk up the mountain, with the thermometer at near 80°, to a considerable height. After traversing impracticable paths for a considerable distance, we gave up the waterfall, though we were repaid by a fine view of the valley, which reminded me of the Devil's Glen in Wicklow, with its tropical products. The damp climate makes this country very verdant, and it seems to be very healthy, considering the amount of rain and the vicinity to the Equator. Europeans, however, require frequent change, which cannot be obtained without travelling long distances. Mrs. Philippo the wife of the Attorney-General of the Straits, had come up in the "Golconda" from Singapore to join her husband, who was in attendance on the Governor here. I called at the Colonial Office to see Mr. Philippo, whom I had known in England. He was not there; but the Governor, Sir William Jervoise, very kindly saw me. He is a pleasing, gentlemanly man, and I felt very sorry for him in the difficulties in which he was involved. I told him I thought a great objection to annexation was, that it would involve a large increase in the European establishment, both civil and military, which was undesirable in such a climate. To this he replied that the climate was exceedingly healthy.

The affairs of the Malay States must occasion great anxiety, both to the Colonial Secretary and to the Governor of the Straits. The East India Company acquired the settlements of Singapore, Malacca, and Penang, which are of great importance to us, on account of our large trade to China. Surrounded, as they are, by a barbarous population of Malays, a population much given to piracy, our relations with the natives must always have required great care. Our course would seem to be to have as little as possible to do with the internal administration of the native States. Interference would be sure to involve us, sooner or later, in wars; and, considering the climate, it is desirable to keep no troops in the Straits of Malacca, except such as are absolutely necessary for the protection of our settlements. No doubt there are difficulties in such a course. A mercantile community is always anxious to use arms in support of their trade, and the constant pressure of colonial society has a tendency to drive a Governor to take steps which a statesman who considers those questions in the calm seclusion of Downing Street finds it difficult to approve. A large immigration of Chinese has, of late years, taken place to the Malay Peninsula, and their conflicts with the natives have complicated the position of affairs. The country appears to be rich in mines, which are a great inducement to English capitalists to settle in it. In 1867 the management of these colonies was transferred from the Indian Government to the Colonial Secretary. Till 1873 the Colonial Office wisely strove to prevent interference with the troubled politics of the native States. Their policy is laid down in a letter from the unfortunate Mr. Birch, Secretary of Sir H. Ord, to the Singapore Chamber of Commerce, dated Singapore, August 21st, 1872,[1] in which he says,—

"At the same time, I am further directed to point out that it is the policy of her Majesty's Government not to interfere in the affairs of these countries, unless where it becomes necessary for the suppression of piracy or the punishment of aggression on our people or territories; and that if traders, prompted by the prospect of large gains, choose to run the risk of placing their persons and property in the jeopardy which they are aware attends them in these countries under present circumstances, it is impossible for Go-

[1] Blue Book, 1874, p. 6.

vernment to be answerable for their protection or that of their property." This letter, which was approved by Lord Kimberley on December 28th,[2] details a policy which might with advantage have been adhered to; but, influenced as it would appear by a petition signed by 248 Chinese merchants, the noble earl altered his views. In a memorable despatch, dated September 20th, 1873,[3] he authorized the Governor to consider "whether any steps could be taken to improve the condition of parts of the peninsula," and suggests the appointment of residents to the native States. This despatch was addressed to the new Governor, Sir Andrew Clarke, who at once proceeded to take steps to regulate the affairs of the native States. Sir Andrew Clarke is a man of great ability, and appears to have acquired much influence over the natives; so that possibly, if he could have remained for a long course of years, some of the evils which have resulted from his proceedings might have been averted. As it was, he accepted what he thought a more desirable appointment in India, and no blame attaches to Sir William Jervoise if he was unable at once to succeed to the influence of his predecessor. As in the case of Ashantee, a change of Governor at a critical moment involved us in war. Sir Andrew Clarke at once proceeded to adjudicate on a disputed succession to the throne of Perak. Ali, the Sultan of Perak, died on the 25th of May, 1871, and a quarrel arose as to his successor. The candidates were Abdullah, one of the

[2] P. 7. [3] P. 38.

royal family, who held an office which had usually been considered to belong to the heir presumptive; and Ismail, who, on Abdullah's failing to attend the funeral of the deceased Sultan, which Malay custom renders imperative on the successor, was placed by the chiefs on the vacant throne. It was argued that Abdullah had been recognized in Sultan Ali's time as his successor, though it was said that his habits and his state of health, probably the result of opium, rendered him unfit to rule. On the other hand, it was claimed for Ismail that, though not of the royal line on his father's side, yet, when his rival failed to fulfil the duty of attending Ali's funeral, he had succeeded to the position, and that his character rendered him far more eligible to govern a wild race. Sir Andrew Clarke decided in favour of Abdullah, and, so far as the Malay law can be gathered from the memoranda of Messrs. Skinner and Irving, given in the Blue Book, the decision was legally justified, though the high authority of Lord Lawrence may be cited to show that it was a mistake. But the more important question arises whether it was wise to interfere at all. Unless both sides were willing to submit to the Governor's arbitration, we should either have to bring British influence into contempt, or to enforce the decision by arms; and our military strength was reduced at the very time when its increase became necessary, owing to the policy of interference. Ismail retained the regalia—a most important matter in this country. With great admiration for Sir A. Clarke, whose acquaintance I had afterwards the pleasure of making at Calcutta, I cannot but think that his interference in the Perak question was most unfortunate.

The other point referred to in Lord Kimberley's despatch was the appointment of Residents at the native Courts. In India, in many of the native States, the Resident, under the name of advice, communicates the commands of the British Government to the nominal Sovereign; but in India the great military power of England renders the smaller princes virtually our dependents. In the peninsula, our small military force, and the inaccessible nature of much of the country, place the native rulers in a very different position, and the Resident at a Court must fulfil duties of a different kind. Hence the sad events of last year.

The success of our troops leaves it open to consider our future policy. The opinion of the colonists strongly supports the annexation of the peninsula, at least with the exception of Johore, whose enlightened ruler has been our faithful ally. This opinion has been maintained in language of folly and absurdity by the colonial press. The objection is obvious that it will involve a large sacrifice of the lives both of civilians and soldiers to the exigencies of residence in a tropical climate. Lord Carnarvon is right to resist, as long as he can, a measure involving such a sacrifice. Still, sooner or later, the consideration must force itself on the British Government whether, after the proceedings of Sir Andrew Clarke, any course remains but the virtual, if not formal, annexation of the country. In these questions it may be easy to avoid a first step, but that step once taken is irrevocable.

Should annexation be forced upon us, it is a satisfaction to remember that, whatever the sacrifice to England, our rule will be a blessing to the native population.

The transfer of the Straits Settlements from the Indian to the Colonial Secretary is a step to be regretted. I have not heard any reason assigned, but I can well suppose that it was a matter of convenience in Downing Street. The responsible government of our great colonies must have lessened the work of the Colonial Secretary, while, on the other hand, that of his Indian colleague must be constantly increasing. Still there must have been many advantages in the connexion of the Straits with India. Indian statesmen are trained to deal with an Asiatic population, and the habits acquired by a Collector must be far more useful to a Governor of the Straits than those of an officer of a scientific corps. The population of the Malay peninsula are much more likely to be understood by a man trained in India than by one imported from the other side of the world. Another consideration is the Army. Should it be necessary, as I fear it may be, to permanently increase our military force at Singapore, there would be a great advantage in maintaining there some Sepoy regiments. It would relieve the English force serving there, and would be a great assistance in maintaining order. It is to be hoped that, whatever the arrangements of the Home Government, Indian experience may in future be more largely employed in the administration of these Settlements.

We left at 3 p.m., and enjoyed the beautiful scenery as we steamed off. The next day we had a heavy storm of rain, which is called here a Sumatra. We passed Atcheen Head, the north point of Sumatra, surrounded by islands. On our starboard was an island called Pulo Rondo, which reminded me of the Steep Holms in the Bristol Channel. Atcheen is a country in which we had claims, which we surrendered to the Dutch in exchange for Elmina. Two wars followed—ours with the King of Ashantee, and that of the Dutch with the Malays of Sumatra. The Dutch have experienced great difficulties in this war, and have been frequently defeated. They seem to be much hated by the Malays, and I was told, though not on particularly good authority, that the origin of our difficulties in Perak might be traced to the surrender of Atcheen. The Malays say we were bound not to give them up, and the disgust of the inhabitants of Sumatra has been reflected by the conduct of their brethren in the peninsula. From Atcheen Head our course was nearly due west for Ceylon. The run of the 19th was 232; 20th, 298; 21st, 298; and 22nd, 266. The thermometer stood at 82° and 83°. The 21st was the shortest day, but we were too near the Equator for this to make much difference. The "Golconda," though an old boat, is a wonderfully good one, and made capital time. On the 22nd we approached Ceylon, and, the night being very dark, we had to go slow and take soundings. Between six and seven next morning, we enjoyed the pretty sight of three P. and O. steamers, from distant ports, meeting and following each other into the harbour of Point de Galle. The "China" from Australia led the way, the "Golconda" followed from Shanghai, and the "Mirzapore" from Calcutta brought up the rear. It shows how well the P. and O. service is regulated. The groves of cocoa-nuts made the scene very charming. Galle is a small harbour, and, when several large ships meet there, there is a competition for the best anchorage. The Prince of Wales has laid the foundation of a breakwater at Colombo, and the people of that city hope, when it is completed, it will supersede Galle. The fact that no effort is made to construct a railway from here to the capital seems to show that the importance of Galle is thought only to be temporary.

After breakfast I landed in a canoe scooped out of the trunk of a tree, and proceeded to the Oriental Hotel. This hotel, which is one of the best in the East, is kept by Mr. Barker, formerly a servant of Alderman Finnis. It was crowded with the passengers of the three boats which had just arrived. An immense verandah before the house is filled with large armchairs to lounge in. Here travellers smoke, while natives crowd round them to exchange money and sell jewellery. You are persecuted by these fellows to an extent I never saw equalled; but as there is little to see, and the heat prevents your moving much about, their pertinacity is rather amusing. I got from the Oriental Bank some of their notes which circulate in the island; saw a wedding at the church; bought a topee or hat to keep off the sun; and took my place by night coach to Colombo. In the afternoon I accompanied Captain Grant on board the "Mirzapore," in which he was going home. I almost wished I was going to accompany him, though I felt that the most interesting and instructive part of my journey still lay before me. The "Mirzapore," which is a very fine boat, was conveying four elephants to the Khedive, for which stalls had been fitted up on deck.

At half-past six, after taking leave of my fellow-passengers, I started in the mail, a covered carriage, Captain Parlby, who was ordered to Colombo, being my fellow-passenger. As far as I could make out, the road ran between groves of palms on one side and the sea on the other. The fire-flies were very pretty. We had supper about half-past eleven at a road-side inn near the sea, and accomplished our journey of seventy-two miles by six next morning. I at once proceeded to the railway station, and took the train for Kandy by the Government railway, distance seventy-four miles. The line first crosses plains covered with cocoa-nuts, bamboos, and other tropical trees, and then traverses a chain of mountains, winding along precipices and overlooking a magnificent scene. Of course snowy mountains are wanting, and there are no lakes in sight, but, as a picture of hill and woodland, I have seldom seen it equalled and never surpassed.

At Kandy I stopped at the Queen's Hotel for Christmas-day and Sunday. Kandy is beautifully situated on a lake surrounded by hills. Excellent roads run round it, while on the side away from the town you may walk for miles over hills covered with coffee and other plantations, which reminded me of those around Mentone. On the other side, behind the Governor's palace, a long succession of rides and walks are carried through lovely woods. After traversing these for some distance you reach a turn in the road overlooking an extensive valley with a fine river running through it. Great pains seem to have been taken in laying out these drives by successive governors, who have associated their names with the different paths. The town itself lies in a valley near the lake and is very straggling. The palace, the church, and the green remind one of an English village, though the streets, filled with swarthy Singalese, dispel the illusion. The population is nearly 17,000. The chief temple is called the Temple of the Sacred Tooth, and is said to contain the tooth of Buddha. I was glad to see several chapels of native Christian congregations scattered about the town. The congregation of the English church seemed principally composed of the military. I was sorry not to find Sir William Gregory, the Governor of Ceylon, at home, but he had gone to Calcutta to meet the Prince of Wales. From what I could learn from those with whom I came in contact, and from the newspapers, there seems to be some difference between him and the planters. Some planters had been recently convicted by the magistrates of ill-treating some coolies, and the planting interest charged the Governor with inducing the justices to inflict an unduly harsh punishment. The story sounded to me an exceedingly improbable one, as Sir William Gregory would not be likely to interfere till the matter came officially before him, and neither governor nor magistrates would inflict a penalty more severe than that which they felt impelled by a sense of duty to award. In countries where the white population depend on coolie labour, there is often a tendency in the authorities to favour the master at the expense of the labourer. Of course, in all communities there are men of different dispositions, and I believe the coffee planters of Ceylon have among them several gentlemen who do honour to their country. A gentleman, who seemed to be a surveyor in the Government service, told me that waste land suitable for coffee is put up at ten rupees an acre as an upset price. When brought into cultivation, the value of the best land sometimes exceeds 100*l.* per acre, but the quantity under cultivation is constantly increased as new land is reclaimed from the hills. The coffee planters had lately been making money fast. The weather was fine during my stay at Kandy, and it was curious on Christmas-day to have windows and doors in church open.

On the 27th I took the railway to Gampola, where, after breakfast, I proceeded by the coach to Rambodde, through a pretty country, which is traversed by a well-made road. At Rambodde several fine waterfalls make the scene beautiful. As the coach stops here, I proceeded to walk up the mountain road to Nuwara Eliya (pronounced Nuralia). This road is one of those wonderful specimens of engineering with which we are so familiar in the Alps, and is carried up the pass by a succession of terraces. The distance from Rambodde to Nuwara Eliya is fourteen miles, the last seven or eight of which I had to travel by the light of the stars. I should have accomplished it very comfortably had it not been that on arriving at Nuwara Eliya the road skirts the town instead of passing through it. The town is, in fact, merely some detached houses. Hence I plodded on till seing "48" on a milestone, when I knew Nuwara Eliya was only forty-seven, I turned into a house where I saw a light to inquire. A Mr. Oldfield received me most hospitably, told me I had come too far by nearly two miles, and sent his son back with me to Hawkins' Club, now an hotel.

Next morning I started at half-past six to ascend Pedro, the highest mountain in Ceylon. It is 8590 feet above the level of the sea; but, as Nuwara Eliya is 6500, there is only about 2000 feet to climb. The horse-path ascends the side of the mountain through woods which extend nearly to the summit. Water is to be found within a short distance of the top—a proof of the moisture of the climate. The summit is marked by a pole on a heap of stones, and commands a very extensive view, which rather reminded me of that from Monte Casino. Nuwara Eliya, situated in a plain, with a pretty though small lake, the hills and woods which surround it, and the chains of mountains stretching away in all directions, form a magnificent panorama. Clouds, which, however, rather enhanced the beauty of the view, prevented the sea being visible. After returning to the hotel (which, for the information of future travellers, I may say was very dear), and resting there through the heat of the day, I started to return to Rambodde by the same road I had traversed the previous evening. Ascending a beautiful glen to the top of the pass, you have a fine view in both directions. For seven miles the road descends along the side of the hill, often in the midst of coffee plantations. The last few miles it is carried down the mountain by terraces, and it is said by short cuts you may save three miles. Being afraid of losing my way, as it was getting dark, I lost much of this advantage. This road may be cited to prove the benefits which British government has conferred on Ceylon. At Rambodde is a rest-house. These rest-houses are houses provided by the Government every few miles, where lodging may be obtained, and where, in the more frequented places, food is provided for travellers. I expected to have found it empty, but to my surprise it was crowded, there being nine at dinner, including a happy couple whom I had seen married at Galle the previous week. A civil engineer present gave me much interesting information about the country. I had walked twenty miles during this day, and eighteen on the previous. Though this would be nothing in Switzerland, even for one who, like myself, is no walker, I thought it pretty good in latitude 7°.

On the morning of the 29th I took a stroll. Rambodde is very beautifully situated on the side of a mountain, surrounded by several fine waterfalls, and commanding a view over a very extensive valley. I returned by mail to Gampola. These Cingalese mails have the privilege, with which, in former days, Englishmen were familiar, that everything is bound to give way to them as belonging to the Queen. It is curious to see a red-turbaned Cingalese blow his horn to warn the bullock-carts to make way for her Majesty's mail. From Gampola I returned to Peradeniya, the station next to Kandy, where I changed into the Colombo train. I reached that city about half-past six, and went to the International Hotel, a temporary building, which is to be replaced by a more permanent one. It had, however, a good supply of English newspapers—a great luxury when you have been long out of the way of news. Colombo, the capital of the island, has a population of 97,129, made up of 55,215 males and of 41,914 females. That of Kandy consists of 10,922 males and 5959 females. The Cingalese are said to destroy their female children, and these figures seem to prove the truth of the statement, and would appear to point to horrible moral evils. The whole population of Ceylon is about 2,400,000, hardly more than that of many collectorates in India. The principal buildings of Colombo, including the Governor's palace and the barracks, are situated on a promontory running out into the sea, marked by a light-house. On one side of this promontory is a large open space, washed by the sea, called Galle Face; on the other the town extends, with a large lake behind it. In this quarter are the cathedral and the law-courts.

Early in the morning of the 30th I enjoyed a bathe,

and afterwards saw a detachment of the 57th Regiment disembark. What struck me was, that the men who had been two years in this hot, wet climate looked more healthy than the troops who were just arriving. It is true the barracks are very good, and everything is done to promote the health of the soldiers; but it would seem the climate is not as unfavourable as one might expect. I lunched with Captain Parlby at the officers' club, where were some officers of a regiment proceeding to the Straits in consequence of the Malay disturbances.

I then called on Sir Comara Swamy, a native barrister here, who was most hospitable, driving me to the Cinnamon Gardens and keeping me to dinner. The party consisted of Sir Comara, who is a Tamil, his nephew, who had been at Cambridge, and a Cingalese gentleman. He complained that the dark races were looked down upon by the white. I told him that I hoped this was not the case, at all events in England; that there are, of course, social distinctions, but the fact that he had been knighted by the Queen placed him above all untitled English gentlemen; and that if black-coloured men were looked down on in the East, it was simply because the large majority were uneducated, and not fitted for refined society. I was sorry afterwards, at Bombay, to find a native merchant excluded from the *table d'hôte*, but this was done, not by an English, but by a Parsee landlord, and when this gentleman embarked on board the "Peshawur" he sat at table next the only passenger on board who had a right to precedence in England. My host spoke highly of the disposition of the Governor to treat the natives justly, and favourably of the planters as a body. I was surprised to hear him say that he thought the climate shortened the lives of the natives, and that they did not live to be as old as people in Europe.

After a very short night, I started by the day-coach to return to Galle in time for the boat to Madras. There is a day as well as a night mail, which travels wonderfully. With wretched screws of horses, they go the pace of the old Cornish Quicksilver Mail—a mile in five minutes and a half. But, though they travel well, they lose an immense time in changing horses. The fresh ones are never ready, and often jib going off. The distance of seventy-two miles takes ten hours and a half; so that, deducting half an hour for tiffin, the pace is little over seven miles an hour, though they drive at the rate of eleven. The road leaves Colombo by Galle Face, and then keeps near the sea, through a succession of groves of cocoa-nut, crossing several rivers. In the latter part it runs along the sea-shore. I was glad to see several small churches, which seemed to belong to the native Christians. But few women are visible in Ceylon. The men have a curious practice of throwing back their hair with combs, in the same way as little girls sometimes do in England. We reached the Oriental Hotel, Galle, at half-past four. At eleven at night there was service at the church in commemoration of the close of the year, where I was glad to see a large congregation, including many soldiers. A service at the conclusion of the year is striking, and the private prayer in which the congregation engaged as midnight approached was very solemn.

January 1, 1876, I spent in Galle, as the Calcutta boat was advertised to sail, but she had not arrived. Galle is very pretty, as the sea is fine and the palm-groves look charming; but the excessive heat (the thermometer was 86°) makes it unpleasant. New Year's Day is observed as a holiday. Both the English and the Presbyterian churches were open, and seemed well attended, both by the white and the Burgher population. The half-castes are here called Burghers. I strolled about the town, made some purchases, and in the afternoon Captain Lavie, of the Royal Artillery, very kindly took me round the ramparts. Galle is a peninsula, being surrounded on three sides by water. He told me that you have to be careful in bathing, on account of the sharks, which are numerous here. I pitied a party of American fellow-passengers who had remained for ten days in this stifling atmosphere, while I had been up the country, where I was very fortunate in not being interfered with by rain. Ceylon is a lovely island, but the luxuriant vegetation shows the quantity of rain which falls. I find by the Ceylon Almanac that between the years 1870 and 1873 the rainfall varied in Colombo from 63 to 107 inches; at Galle, from 67 to 77; at Kandy, from 69 to 97; at Nuwara Eliya, from 75 to 107; and, at a hill station whose name I forget, from 155 to 170. There are, however, places in India where the fall is much greater. Newman's

Indian Bradshaw states that "hotel charges throughout Ceylon are very high." With the exception of Nuwara Eliya, I did not find this to be the case. Coach-fares, however, are high compared to England. From Colombo to Galle is 22½ rupees, from Gampola to Rambodde 10 rupees. The Government railway is said to be paying well, and the planters are anxious it should be extended further into the coffee districts. On the morning of Sunday, the 2nd, the "Surat," Captain Byrne, from Aden, arrived. The arrangement is that the boats from Southampton to Calcutta, and from Bombay to Shanghai, meet at Galle to transfer passengers, and this transference is one of the great complaints made in China against the P. and O. The monthly mail-boat to and from Australia also communicates here. The "Gwalior," from Bombay, owing to an accident to her machinery, only arrived about two hours before we sailed. I went on board the "Surat" about half-past three, and found a pleasant set of passengers *en route* for India, including Colonel Denison, brother of the late Speaker. On the 3rd we had some heavy tropical storms of rain. We saw the mountains and sandy coast in the morning, and passed some boats engaged in constructing a lighthouse off Basses' Rocks. In the afternoon we lost sight of Ceylon. It is said that "happy is the country which has no history," and I do not recollect that for more than a quarter of a century anything has occurred to call public attention to the affairs of this beautiful and interesting island. Under the government of Lord Torrington, about 1848, some disturbances occurred, but since that period Ceylon has had an uneventful history. It is to be hoped that its material prosperity may continue and increase, and still more that, under God's blessing, Christian missions may be largely blessed. The distance from Galle to Madras is 545 miles. The "Surat" is not a fast boat, but on the night of the 4th she had to slow her engines not to arrive before daylight.

CHAPTER V.

MADRAS AND SOUTHERN INDIA.

On waking on the morning of January 5th I found we were at anchor in Madras Roads. The town looked imposing from the sea, though, with the exception of Fort St. George, the principal buildings were not visible. It is a striking sensation to be for the first time in sight of that land whose conquest by a company of English merchants is among the most marvellous events in the history of the world. The mind turns to those great men, both soldiers and statesmen, whose genius and energy have subdued this wonderful country, and we should also do justice to those Christian heroes who have devoted and often sacrificed their lives to proclaim the Gospel of peace to the vast heathen population.

After breakfast we landed, passing through the surf in boats sewed together, and rowed by ten coolies each. The day was not rough, but, when it is so, landing must be dangerous, and occasionally steamers have had to leave without being able to put their passengers on shore. It is said to be a curious sight to see a newly-arrived governor landing amid tho rejoicing of the population, and, with thunders of artillery, hauled on shore from these boats in anything but a dignified manner. The Prince of Wales wisely landed at the southern port of Tuticorin, and entered Madras by railway. Of all the wonderful displays I heard described in connexion with his Royal Highness's journey, one of the most beautiful must have been the lighting up of the surf at Madras. The great southern capital of India consists of a number of small towns and villages, twenty-three in all, scattered over an area of twenty-seven square miles. The principal are—Black Town, of which the first part has a population of 65,000, the second of 75,000; Triplicaine, with 60,000; and St. Thomas, with 41,000. The population of the whole municipality is nearly 400,000. Black Town stands on the shore, with Fort St. George to the south. The country behind looks like a collection of bungalows placed in a great park.

I had gone to the Elphinstone Hotel, but, on calling on the Duke of Buckingham, he most kindly invited me to Government House, where I was treated with unbounded hospitality by himself, his daughters, and his staff. The most interesting spot in Madras is Fort St. George, which, like the 39th Regiment, might claim "the proud motto, *Primus in Indus.*" Here the Company had a trading-factory; here Clive came out as a clerk; and here that great genius was developed which was destined to lay the foundation of British supremacy in India. It is still the seat of the Madras Government, where the Council sits, and the official business is transacted. Here I was introduced to Mr. Huddlestone, the Secretary to the Government, who gave me some very interesting information about the land, revenue, tanks, &c. He is the third generation of his family who has served in India, his father and grandfather having both preceded him. The system by which the sons of old Indians came to India, possessing a basis of knowledge of the country, was a great advantage of the Company's rule—an advantage we are in danger of losing under competition. Mr. Huddlestone, however, did not seem to regret the change, saying India had gone on improving both under the Company and under the Queen. I was shown the arsenal by two very distinguished officers, Colonel Caddell and Colonel Campbell, the chiefs of the Madras artillery. Here the old standards of many native regiments are suspended, and the keys of Pondicherry are shown. Colonel Caddell told me that he received the Governor of Pondicherry here, and that he said to him, "I wish you would give us up those keys." The Colonel replied, "We will do it with pleasure on one condition, that you give us in return the keys of Madras, which you keep in Paris." The capture of Madras by the French, and of Pondicherry by the English, took place in the wars between the English and French East India Companies in the days of Clive and Dupleix. The cathedral contains a monument to Daniel Corrie, one of the Company's chaplains, who laboured as a missionary in India, and died the first Bishop of Madras. I visited the Museum, which contains a large collection of Indian curiosities, the public gardens and the people's park. At the Moncgar Choultry is a native charity, which provides for lepers, incurables, and those who are afflicted in other ways, and which appears a very useful institution. The managers, like every one else here, are appointed by the Government. It seems a pity that greater efforts are not made to train the people in habits of self-government. A bill was under discussion for the creation of a municipal council for Madras, of which half were to be elected and half nominated by the Government, thus keeping the control with the Government.

Though the principal offices of administration are at Fort St. George, Government House is situated about a mile and a half inland. It is a large building in Indian style, standing in a pretty park. The walls are adorned with portraits of governors and native princes connected with the history of the Presidency. Dinner-parties are given in a large hall, with its sides open to the air, which makes it very pleasant in this climate. About six miles from Madras is Gindy, where the country palace of the Governor is situated, surrounded by beautiful gardens. It is a curious arrangement that the Governor, having two large residences close to each other, is obliged to hire houses for himself and his suite at Ootacamund, where he spends great part of the year. It seems wonderful that they do not sell Gindy, and buy a place at Ootacamund with the proceeds, though perhaps it might not be an easy place to dispose of. Near Gindy is Mount

St. Thomas, so called from a tradition which, however, is generally discredited, that the Apostle Thomas was martyred here. Captain Hadaway, the Duke's aide-de-camp, drove me here, and showed me the barracks, which are very comfortable. On both the days I was at Government House I met large parties at dinner, including many of the leading men at Madras. The Presidency was spared the horrors of the mutiny, though some of my friends told me of the terror which they experienced at the time. The Mohammedans are not numerous in the south, and the Hindoo population, as a rule, remained quiet. It is true the Bengal sepoys revolted, influenced by the chupatties, but the feeling thus engendered was taken advantage of by the Mohammedans. The Hindoos for a long succession of ages have been ruled by others, and they feel that the English sway has been more peaceful and more beneficial to them than those which preceded it. They know that all they can expect is a change of masters, and though they may not like the English, they are not anxious to upset them. The Mussulmen, on the other hand, have the angry feeling that we displaced them from the rule of India. They resent our having deposed a Mohammedan line of sovereigns, and though they may not expect to re-establish one of their princes at Delhi, they at least hate the nation which has dethroned the Mogul. We sometimes hear it said that our alliance with Turkey is a great assistance to us in securing the allegiance of the Mussulmen of India. This statement is made in England, but I never heard it sanctioned by any one in India of whom I asked the question. It is to be borne in mind that a large proportion of the Mohammedans in India are Shiis, who hate the Turks, and it is not likely that they will be influenced by sympathy for the Sultan, whom they do not regard as the legitimate Caliph.

The great anxiety at Madras appeared to be the inefficient way in which the native army is officered. In the days of the Company there used to be twenty-eight officers to a native regiment, who now are reduced to seven. Even these are often not with the regiment, and the Sepoys are left to two or three officers. In case of war, vacancies would be filled up from the staff corps, but officers pitchforked into a regiment cannot possess the affections of the men, and the bond of attachment which bound the Sepoy to his officer in the olden time exists no longer. Complaints are made that the services are all trying to get as much pay and as much leave as they can, and that the present generation are not possessed of that knowledge of India and that zeal for the public service which distinguished their predecessors. This may be partly owing to the increased means of communication with home. When the voyage from England to India was an affair of six, sometimes of twelve months, men settled more completely among the people, and acquired a knowledge of native languages and native customs, such as now is rare, but at least it is to be wished that the officials of the present day should be alive to the immense responsibilities involved in our position.

The Duke most kindly sketched me out a route for seeing the antiquities of Southern India to the greatest advantage in the time at my disposal. Before my return he had gone with Lady Ann Grenville and Lady Anna Gore-Langton, on a visit to the Godavery, to enable him to judge for himself of the public works necessary in connexion with that river. The national gratitude is eminently due to the Duke of Buckingham for the great sacrifices which he and his family are making in the public service. To most men the position of Governor of Madras would be an object of honourable ambition, but to one who has filled the still higher position of Secretary of State, with advantage to his sovereign and with honour to himself, to say nothing of his possessing the highest rank in the Peerage, it can present no attractions. He is the first statesman of cabinet rank who has accepted an Indian appointment less than the Viceroyalty, while many Viceroys have not attained to such a position in England. The Government of Madras cannot add to the dignity which under any circumstances he enjoys at home, while to his daughters it must be an exile, but the circumstance of his undertaking it must be of the greatest benefit to India. It shows the princes and people of the great Eastern Empire that British statesmen are ready, at every sacrifice of personal comfort, to devote their lives to the promotion of the interests of our great dependency.

On the evening of the 7th I left Madras with introductions for the provinces from Captain Hankin, the Governor's Secretary. Major Hobart, his colleague, who was going on the Godavery expedition, very kindly saw me off at the station. The Indian railway carriages are exceedingly comfortable, and you are able to sleep in berths as you do in America. The fares are one-and-a-half anna per mile, first class; three-quarter anna, second class. As sixteen annas make a rupee, it will be seen that first class fares are a little dearer, second class a little cheaper than in England, or rather were so while the rupee was two shillings. The depreciation in silver will change this, like a good many other things. The natives travel third class, and in the North there is also what is called "intermediate class." We dined at Arconum Junction, where the line to Bombay is left, and passed Arcot and Vellore, places memorable in the early history of British India. Much as I had enjoyed Madras, the heat had been so great that I had not slept well, and finding it cooler in the train, I overslept myself. I was not roused at the Erode Junction Station, where I ought to have changed carriages for Trichinopoly. At a little place called Watkallee, some twenty miles beyond Erode, I had to wait for a train to take me back. The mistake lost me the day for sight-seeing, but I was not sorry to see something of India in a way I should not have done except by accident. Watkallee is a small station on a plain, with distant hills in sight. The roads around are good, having aloes for hedges on either side. At Erode the South Indian leaves the Madras Railway, running to Trichinopoly, whence one line is carried to Tuticorin, another to Negapatam. The fares on these lines are very cheap, though they do not give return tickets. The ride to Trichinopoly was through a country with pleasing views, though it frequently looked parched. The trains on this line travel slowly, stopping at every station. The last part of the journey I fell in with some Brahmins, who talked good English, and were very civil, bringing in a fiddler to play to me. The language of this part of India is Tamil, but to the North of Madras Telugu is spoken. The military language is Hindustanee, which is generally used in the army. English is generally understood, to a certain extent, by the Madras servants.

We reached Trichinopoly in the evening, where I was most hospitably entertained by Mr. and Mrs. Sewell. Mr. Sewell is the collector of a district comprising 5000 square miles, which is not considered a large one. At dinner I met several officers, who spoke strongly about the deficiency of officers to the Native Army. The 9th was Sunday. The principal service here is in the evening. It is curious to be obliged to have punkas in church, but the heat is great, and the trying part of it must be that it continues all the year round. Trichinopoly is associated with the early history of Clive. It belonged to a prince who was in alliance with the English, but who was besieged by the French. Clive's heroic defence at Arcot gave him time to resist them, and he was ultimately relieved by the British leader. The palace at Trichinopoly had been handsomely fitted up for the reception of the Prince of Wales, and the town was full of triumphal arches erected to welcome him. His visit appeared to have given great pleasure to the natives, though several towns in the Madras Presidency were disappointed at not seeing him, as his visit was cut short, owing to an alarm of cholera. It was generally said by the Europeans that this alarm was unnecessary; and I was told by Dr. Fox, a medical officer in the army, who very kindly took me to the Rock, that in fifteen years' professional experience, he had only known three or four Englishmen die from this complaint. It certainly seemed extraordinary that the Prince should have been advised not to visit the Neilgherries, the great health resort of South India. It was often amusing to read the lucubrations of the *Lancet* on the subject, which were copied into the Indian papers. Still, it must be remembered, in justice to the Prince's medical adviser, that at the time of his visit cholera did, to a certain extent, prevail in the South among the poorer natives; and a sepoy who marched past his Royal Highness at Madura died the same day.

Dr. Fox showed me a well-managed hospital, the prison, and the sacred tank. The Rock Temple is the great object of interest at Trichinopoly. The Rock rises to the height of 200 feet, with temples both on the sides and on the summit, the abode of sacred monkeys. It is ascended by flights of steps, and commands a very extensive view over immense plains, sometimes lost in the distance, often verdant with palms, with rocky hills rising in different directions, while the sacred stream of the Cavary flows beneath. In some respects it reminded me of the view from Milan Cathedral, though the arid tropical country is a contrast to the verdant plains of Lombardy. Some two miles beyond the Rock, on the other side of the river, is situated the great Temple of Srirungam, covering an enormous space. Seven walls surround the great shrine of Vishnu, and between the fourth and seventh a population of some 10,000 souls resides. Standing on the roof which covers the inner part of the temple, fourteen splendid pagodas are visible rising round the sacred shrine. The scene, looking over these magnificent pagodas, is very imposing, especially from a tower near the gate. Eight great horses, carved in stone, were partly hidden by preparations for a festival shortly expected. Notices were circulated by Mr. Sewell on behalf of the Government, warning pilgrims that there was a risk of cholera in visiting Srirungam. I was shown over the temple by the native doctor of an excellent dispensary which is established here, who told me he belonged to the Sudra caste.

I devoted the 10th to an excursion to Tanjore. Starting very early, after a journey of about thirty miles, I reached what Macaulay calls "the rich rice-fields of Tanjore," where I was kindly entertained by Mr. Burnell, the judge. Tanjore was the chief town of the Chota kingdom of South India, and is first heard of about 250 B.C. Chota, Chira, and Pandya were then the three great kingdoms of the South. After various fortunes and conquests by the Cera and Pandya kings, the Chota kingdom revived about 900 A.D. Tanjore then became the chief city, and in the eleventh century the great temple there was built, and the irrigation works of the district were finished. In the beginning of the fourteenth century the Mohammedans invaded South India, and the old Chota kingdom fell. Soon after this the Tanjore province was conquered by the Telugu sovereigns of Viyayanagara (near Bellary), and a branch of the family established itself at Tanjore in the latter half of the fourteenth century. These kings are called the Telugu Nayakas, and built the Tanjore palace. About 1674 the Mahrattas conquered Tanjore, and held it under the Mohammedan nabobs of Arcot till 1799. The Mahratta family became extinct in the male line about 1855, when the town was taken over by the East India Company, one of the instances of that annexation policy of Lord Dalhousie which produced the mutiny.

The palace is very extensive, and contains two fine halls for durbars. Some gorgeous jewelled dresses of the Rajahs are shown. It possesses a very valuable collection of Sanscrit MSS., of which Mr. Burnell, who is one of the greatest of Sanscrit scholars, is engaged in making a catalogue. The temple is dedicated to Siva, and is very magnificent. Several pagodas rise out of a vast enclosure, surrounded by a high wall. Being open, it is seen to much better advantage than some others. The inscriptions, both on the walls and on the stones in the court, are very numerous. It seems a pity that care should not be taken to have them accurately copied, as they are suffering from time and neglect, and much interesting and important historical information might probably be obtained from them. I was much interested in visiting Mr. Burnell's court. Both in it and in that of his sub-judge, who is a Brahmin, it was curious to see turbaned Hindoos pleading in English. The people have an uncommon fondness for litigation, and those who practise show great legal ability. The obstinacy with which disputed causes are carried from one tribunal to another is remarkable. I had an interesting conversation with the sub-judge, who was a fine specimen of a Brahmin. Mr. Burnell told me that he was a very good lawyer, and, being a rich man, he liked English rule because it protected his property. He spoke of the condition of Hindu widows, who are not allowed to re-marry, and said they continued in the families of their late husbands, and were generally kindly treated. From Englishmen I heard a different account of their condition. Very young girls are often married to old men, and left widows while little more than children. In olden times they burnt themselves on their husband's pyre. This we have most properly prevented. All honour to the memory of Lord William Bentinck for so doing. But we cannot control the Hindu law which prohibits re-marriage. What wonder if these poor creatures, seeing nothing before them but a blighted existence and menial drudgery little removed from slavery, take to evil courses. At tiffin I met Dr. Hoffmann, Professor of Sanscrit in the University of Madras, and Dr. Hendon, Physician to the Rajah of Travancore. The Rajah had just returned from attending the Prince's Durbar at Calcutta. Dr. Hendon spoke highly of Sir Madova Rao's administration of Travancore. I was sorry to find among Europeans so much distrust of the natives, and so great an indisposition to confide any authority to them. I returned in the evening to Trichinopoly, after a pleasant day, and on the following morning after my visit to Srirungam proceeded to Madura. It was at Trichinopoly that Heber, one of the greatest of Indian Bishops and of English Christian poets, closed his life.

The railways beyond Trichinopoly have a narrow gauge of about 3½ feet. Some people doubt the wisdom of this narrow gauge, and, considering the disadvantage of changing carriages and waggons, and the level nature of the country through which it is constructed, it may be a question whether it was real economy. The line to Madura runs through some pretty wooded hills, which remind one of England. It passes Dindigul, a fortress the English took from Tippoo Sahib. At Madura I was very kindly received by Mr. Bliss, the Collector, who I found came from my own neighbourhood in Wiltshire. Colonel Tait, who had been arranging about the Prince's visit, and Dr. Jago, a German ethnologist, were stopping with him. The temple of Siva at Madura is said to be the finest in South India, though it is not as large as Srirungam. It was begun before the Christian era, and not finished till 1459. It is kept in excellent repair, and is distinguished by the elaborate carving for which the natives are remarkable. It has a hall called the hall of one thousand columns (the real number being 999) several pagodas rising above it, and some fine corridors. The goddess Menukshi seems the principal object of worship here, and her figure is constantly seen. Improvements and additions, particularly in carved figures, are still made here. This was one of the temples which in former times the English Government took charge of. It was argued that we were bound to respect the religious feelings of the natives, and that in taking care that the funds belonging to the temples were devoted to their legitimate object, we gave no sanction to idolatry; that the priests were apt to misappropriate money committed to their hands; and that the supervision of these edifices by British officials not only gave satisfaction to our subjects, but was a security for the honest employment of the revenues of large districts. On the other hand, it was urged that it was wrong for the representatives of a Christian nation to connect themselves with the degrading superstitions and immoral and often cruel practices with which the Hindoo worship is inseparably associated; that we could not superintend such ceremonies without leaving in the minds of the natives the feeling that religion was a matter of indifference to us; and that it became us to withdraw from all complicity with a system so opposed to our most solemn convictions. This subject was long discussed in Leadenhall-street, but at length the party long led by Mr. Grant, supported by public opinion out of doors, carried the day. It was determined that the Company should relinquish all connexion with the temples, that the revenues of the lands belonging to them should be handed over to the Brahmins, and that, except in deciding disputes which may come before them in their judicial capacity, British officials should refrain from all interference. This decision, arrived at in 1841, does honour to the East India Company.

It is in the South that the great monuments of the Hindoo religion are to be found. With the exception of Benares, of which the temples, though very numerous, are not large, the chief buildings of the North are Mohammedan. Agra, Delhi, and Lucknow are Mohammedan cities, but the tide of conquest left the religion of the great masses of the people of the South unaffected. Here are to be found the magnificent shrines of Vishnu and Siva, as it is remarkable that temples are hardly ever dedicated to Brahma.

The palace is an enormous building, which has latterly fallen into decay, but is now being fitted up for government offices. Here, as everywhere else, one saw the remains of the preparations for the Prince's visit. The natives appear to have subscribed most liberally to welcome with becoming splendour their future sovereign. He stopped at a house which was fitted up for him, close to a beautiful tank, erected by the native princes. The walls are of solid masonry, and in the middle is an island surmounted by a pagoda.

in the midst of palm-trees. Although the day in India begins very early, yet the necessity of keeping in-doors during the heat makes the time for sight-seeing limited. You rise at daybreak (I was told regiments are on parade at the earliest dawn), and take what is called a chota hazi, which consists of tea, toast, and perhaps an egg. You then go out, walking or riding, and return to breakfast at nine or ten. You spend the day in the shade, taking a heavy tiffin at two, drive out at five, and return at dark, dining about eight. They say it is necessary to live high in such a climate; and of course experience is the best guide, though I should have thought the enormous tiffins *de trop*. They do not indulge in siestas, for which in fact officials have no time. A collector's verandah is crowded with peons and other natives. The number of servants kept is enormous. I was reminded of the remark of the Rev. Henry Martyn on landing at Madras, that the Madrassees "seemed to think they were born to wait on the English." It is wonderful at how cheap a rate the natives seem to live. The wages of a groom are six rupees a month, and many of the natives, those who pull the punkas, for instance, get much less. On the other hand, every horse has not only a groom but a grass-cutter, a woman, often the wife of the groom, who gets four rupees per month.

The collector of a district is a little king in it. He is responsible for the collection of the revenues, and is besides a magistrate, though for heavy offences a judge is separately deputed for each district. His power is great over the condition of the district; and Macaulay said very truly, that the personal character of a collector was of more importance to the happiness of probably a million of natives than the difference between the best and the worst Government we ever have in this country to that of the people of England. The revenue system in Madras is mostly the ryotwarree, by which the land belongs to the ryot, subject to a rent to the Government. Thus the collector comes in contact with the ryots, or small native proprietors. A complaint is made that Madras has to contribute more than its fair share to the revenues of India; and certainly the large rent paid by the ryots is one of those things which are to be regretted, but which in the present state of the finances of India there seems no way to alter. Civilians take their choice between the revenue and judicial branches of the service, which are kept distinct.

The three gentlemen whom I here visited are all Oxford graduates, and belong to the early days of competition for the Indian civil service. When first instituted, competition secured the best men from the Universities for India. It is much to be regretted that more recently a set of professional crammers have coached their pupils to carry off a large number of these appointments. Hence it is to be feared that the more recently appointed civilians are not calculated to maintain the high reputation and great traditions of the service.

I accompanied Dr. Jago and Colonel Tait in the evening to see a temple procession. We drove into the town in a bandy, drawn by two bullocks, which travelled at a good pace, and met the procession coming from the temple of Vishnu. It was led off by two elephants, a large and a small, the difference of their height forming a ridiculous contrast. Musicians were seated on their backs, beating their drums, while dancing-girls followed behind. Then came the figure of the god seated in a car and borne by men. Boys with torches surrounded the procession, though it was full moon. Garlands were presented to the spectators, and hung round their necks. The idol was borne through the streets, which were crowded with natives, and carried round a sacred tank, after which we returned to the temple, where one of the Nautch girls danced. The words of their songs are said to be very indecent, but the dance itself appeared harmless enough. Still the whole ceremony was a mournful exhibition of a nation wandering in heathen darkness. I regretted that time did not permit my visiting Tinnevelly, which is situated in this part of India, where the preaching of the Gospel has been so greatly blessed.

At half-past five on the morning of the 13th I left Madura, Mr. Bliss accompanying me as far as Dindigul. He told me that his district has nearly as large a population and half as large an area as Ceylon. This is an illustration of the great power wielded by the Indian Civil Service. The government of Ceylon is one of the most coveted appointments in the gift of the Crown. At the present moment it is held by one who for a long course of years was an influential member of Parliament, and who on quitting Westminster was made a Privy Councillor. An Indian collector is almost unknown outside his own presidency; and yet probably the collector has as much or more power to influence the welfare and happiness of the population under his care. It is true he is responsible to the Governor; but as long as the revenue is regularly remitted and the province is quiet, this responsibility amounts to little. The ryots, if they had cause for complaint, have not the means of making themselves heard. The Governor of Ceylon, on the other hand, is surrounded by Europeans, and subject to the criticism of the press, which is sure to bring to light any errors or shortcomings. These considerations show the immense importance of maintaining the high character of the Civil Service.

My route was over ground that I had previously traversed. I lunched at Trichinopoly, and stopped for the night at Erode, where I was fortunate enough to fall in with Mr. Molesworth, the Government Inspector of Railways, who gave me some interesting information about the Indian lines.

Next morning I again set off at half-past five for Ootacamund, in the Neilgherries, the great sanatorium of the Madras Presidency. Following the main line from Madras to Beypoor as far as Pothanoor junction, where you change trains, and, passing Coimbatore, you reach Metapollium, where the rail ceases. The inhabitants of Ootacamund advocate its continuance, and assert that the heavy charges up the ghaut now paid by travellers would constitute a good dividend on the outlay. Considering, however, the great engineering difficulties of a line up the mountain, I think the supreme government are right to hesitate before they guarantee it. Driving to Salar, at the foot of the Ghaut, I mounted a pony, and rode for ten miles up a lovely pass. The sides are decked with luxuriant vegetation, while you occasionally catch glimpses of the immense plains below. When clouds are floating about the tops of the mountains it adds another charm to the scene. There are very large coffee and some tea plantations among these hills. At the beautiful village of Conoor, distinguished by large barracks, the top of the pass is reached. Here I had some trouble about ponies. I had paid a swindling Mohammedan for ponies to Ooty, but the only one produced at Conoor had no shoes. Ultimately I had to take a carriage. At Conoor the tropical vegetation ceases, and the road to Ootacamund (contracted to Ooty) is comparatively dull, passing over bleak hills and downs with little wood. Ootacamund is a straggling village, or rather collection of villages, reminding one of the little towns in the Cotswolds, which one visits in hunting with the Duke of Beaufort. It is 7300 feet above the level of the sea, and after the heat of Ceylon and Madras it was delicious to reach a place where one had fires instead of punkas, and was not obliged to be up at daybreak if one wanted to walk or ride. Here I was most kindly received by Mr. Cockerell, the commissioner. The hospitality of India, and particularly of Madras, is unbounded. The residents receive travellers, and treat them with the greatest friendship and kindness. In the more frequented cities of the North, owing to the great increase of travelling, it would be impossible to maintain the former system, and hotels, more or less comfortable, are to be everywhere found; but in the South the English maintain the old standard of munificent hospitality. Mr. Cockerell is commissioner, combining the duties of collector and judge. He took me to dine with Colonel Hankin, the brother of Captain Hankin, the Duke's secretary; and I remained with him the two following days. He was one of the Company's writers, educated at Haileybury, a race which is now rapidly leaving India, though the leading Indian statesmen still belong to it. He said there was a disposition, whenever he retired, to make Ootacamund a second-class appointment. To this he objected. It would certainly seem desirable to have a civilian of position in office at a place where the Madras government pass much of the year.

I visited the government chinchona plantations, under the care of Mr. MacIvor, which extend for a considerable distance along the sides of the hills, and then rode round the lake (which was low at the time), a curious winding sheet of water. My host took me to the Lawrence Asylum for soldiers' children, founded by Sir Henry Lawrence, in which he is much interested. It educates upwards of 300 boys, besides a neighbouring school for sixty girls. The boys are brought up to various trades, such as telegraphy, tailoring, carpentering, &c. They are mostly half-castes, who seem badly situated, as they are not received into the Queen's army on the one hand, or into the Native regiments on the other. There are obvious reasons for their not serving in the regular army, for though that army is much in India, yet it is liable to have to serve in cold climates; but it seems a pity that the sons of soldiers, educated in a semi-military school, should not be utilized for her Majesty's service. Mrs. Dene, the wife of the principal, told me they had to send their children home to England to be educated. If this is necessary in the healthy climate of the Neilgherries, it shows how indispensable it is in the parched plains below. Separation from children must be the great trial of Indian life, and England owes a deep debt of gratitude to those who devote their lives to the service of their country in an Eastern exile. Mr. Dene, who is chaplain as well as principal, has large farms and workshops connected with the institution under his care. The production of chinchona, coffee, and tea is carried on largely among the Neilgherries. Complaints are made that the taxation is too great, and that it is a great hindrance to the progress of the country. I was told that so large a royalty was asked on a gold-mine that its working had to be abandoned. I was further told that the taxation of the ryots is too heavy. In good seasons the land tax may be reasonable enough, but in bad it is so severe that it occasionally drives land out of cultivation.

Had time permitted, I should have liked to proceed from Ooty to Mysore, thence visited the fortress of Seringapatam, and returned to Madras by the great military station of Bangalore. To do this would have involved correspondence with Bangalore and Mysore about arrangement for horses, and it is necessary to be very careful not to travel at night, as the road lies through jungles, which are in places very unhealthy. It was just before my journey that the unfortunate Lord Hastings had died at Tanjore. He had been shooting on the Malabar coast, and had traversed a district which those who know the country regard as deadly. This brought on the illness which detained him at Tanjore, where he died. His death shows the necessity of consulting those who are able to advise as to the safety of any particular excursion before undertaking it. With proper arrangements, I understood the journey to Mysore might be undertaken with perfect safety. The great object is to see the fortress of Seringapatam, the capital of Hyder Ali and Tippoo Sahib, which remains much in the same state as when three-quarters of a century ago it fell before the prowess of Harris and Wellesley.

On the 17th I took leave of my hospitable friend, and pushed down the ghaut to Metapollium. The carriage-road is four miles longer than the mule-path, and even more beautiful. It is terraced down the ghaut, and goes through extensive coffee plantations. For some time past coffee-planting has been exceedingly profitable. I was told that the coolies on the plantations were well treated, and that if such were not the case it would be impossible for the planters to get labour. This I was very glad to hear. After a beautiful though dusty ride, during which I was occasionally hindered by meeting long lines of bandies, drawn by bullocks, I reached Metapollium, where I took the train for Madras. At Jollerputt, which is the junction for Bangalore, we had a long detention in the middle of the night, owing to a break-down on the Bangalore line.

In the train I heard a complaint made of the Viceroy, that he had tried to appoint a Brahmin to a collectorship on the Godavery. The appointment was not completed, but, according to my informant, had it been so, the collector would have been murdered by the Mohammedans, who hate the Brahmins. The story seems to me problematical, as collectors are not appointed by the Viceroy, but by the Governors and Lieutenant-Governors of the provinces, but it illustrates the feeling of English society in India. The great statesmen who are at the head of affairs in India feel the importance of conciliating the natives. They know that 100,000 Englishmen cannot permanently keep 250,000,000 of Asiatics in subjection by the sword, and that we ought not only to treat them with justice, but to attach them to us, by enabling them to share in the administration of public affairs; that our motto should be—

> "Tros Tyriusque mihi nullo discrimine agetur."

On the other hand, the lower ranks of the service maintain that, having earned their places by competition, certain advantages are guaranteed to them by Act of Parliament, and that it is a want of faith to them to allow the natives to share these advantages.

This alienation between the English and the natives is one of the great difficulties of the Government of India. The caste system tends to keep up this alienation, as, when men decline to eat at the same table, the difficulties of keeping up friendly intercourse are increased. It is sometimes made a reproach to the English that we can do nothing without a dinner, and of course dinners are liable to abuse; but in these days, when excess in drinking is happily uncommon on such occasions, dinners do much to bind together the different classes of society in one common feeling of friendship. Whether it be in the guilds of the City of London, or at some provincial market town, you see noblemen of ancient lineage and statesmen of parliamentary renown sitting at the same table, associating and mixing with the people. In India caste makes such a state of things impossible. A Sudra may be a powerful chieftain, a Brahmin a common labourer, but the Brahmin will not eat the meat of the Sudra, while the Sudra will not share the food of the Feringhee. Even Scindiah, though not a Hindoo of high caste, when he entertained the Prince of Wales at Gwalior, confined himself to entering the banquet-hall after dinner, and proposing the healths of her Majesty and the Prince. This is one of the great difficulties of intercourse between Englishmen and Hindoos.

Early in the morning I reached Madras. The Duke was absent on his journey to the Godavery, but I was again most kindly entertained at Government House by Lady Mary and Lady Caroline Grenville, where I was fortunate enough to fall in with Sir William Gregory, whom I had known as M.P. for the County Galway, and who is now Governor of Ceylon In the afternoon we went out to Gindy, where the gardens looked beautiful. We dined by the light of hanging lamps under the trees, which made the scene look striking. Sir William, Captain Hankin, and Captain Hadaway started after dinner for an excursion to the "Seven Pagodas." They kindly invited me to accompany them, but I was obliged to return to Madras to await the Calcutta steamer. The 19th was my last day at Madras. I rose at half-past four, and started at five for the Mount, with Captain Aylmer, the Duke's aide-de-camp, and Captain Thackwell, aide-de-camp to Sir W. Gregory, to a meet of the Madras hounds. They meet at the earliest dawn to hunt jackals. They had a good run, and killed, bu as I unluckily came to grief, I did not see much of it. We got back to breakfast, which Lady Mary had kindly put off from nine to ten o'clock. This is an illustration of the Indian plan of taking the day's exercise early in the morning, on tea and toast, and eating three heavy meals during the day afterwards.

In the afternoon I took leave of my friends, who had done so much to make me remember, not only Madras, but Southern India with pleasure, and, taking a boat at the pier, embarked on the "Bokhara," Captain W. D. Anderson, which sailed at 5 p.m. At dinner-time the towers of Fort St. George were being lost in the distance, and we took leave of the capital of Southern India. During my stay I had travelled over 1300 miles. Ootacamund is three hundred and fifty-five from Madras, Trichinopoly is ninety from Erode, Tanjore is thirty-one, and Madura ninety-six from Trichinopoly. The railway system of Madras seems well managed. It is curious that in order to proceed to Calcutta the choice is either to take the steamer or to go round nearly to Bombay. One would have thought that one of the first lines projected in India would have been from Madras to Calcutta, but the rivers running into the Bay of Bengal interpose such great engineering difficulties that such a railway seems to be a vision of the distant future. The want of good harbours on the eastern coast of the peninsula is one of the remarkable features of India which makes it difficult to communicate with populous districts. Hence the frequency of disastrous famines in the eastern provinces.

The question I heard most commonly and most anxiously discussed in Madras was the state of the native army, and the question arises, not only in this presidency, but in other parts of India, whether the state of the sepoy troops is satisfactory. In every point of view this subject is of the utmost importance. Situated as we are, it is necessary to keep up a large military force, while, on the other hand, in the state of the finances it is indispensable to keep our army estimates as low as is consistent with safety. In 1857 the Company's sepoys broke out in that fearful mutiny, which was only suppressed at an immense sacrifice of blood and treasure. Are the present regiments more likely to be faithful to the Queen than their predecessors to the Company? The Company's regiments were fully officered. "We considered the regiment as our home," said an old officer, who was discussing the question, to me. Officers knew their men, talked to them in their own language, took an interest in their pursuits, and, in return, were beloved by the sepoys. Complaints were made in the last years of the Company that the number of English officers was unduly reduced. It was said that the ablest and best officers were often taken away from their regiments and placed in civil employments. The mutiny ensued, and the fact that a conspiracy which must have been known to thousands and tens of thousands should have been kept a secret from the English is certainly one of the most astounding, if not the most astounding event in history. The Sicilian Vespers is the only event to which it can be compared, and the Sicilian Vespers was a conspiracy comparatively on a very small scale. It behoved the British Government to consider how far a native army was required, and what were the best races of Hindostan from which to recruit it. There can be no question that a certain proportion of native troops are necessary. The debilitating effect of the climate of India on European constitutions makes it important to save the English soldier every exertion which is not indispensable. English regiments should, as much as possible, be kept in reserve at hill stations, and, when employed from necessity in the plains, they should be spared exposure to the heat. Hence a native army is an indispensable necessity. Moreover, it must be remembered that the sepoy had stood shoulder to shoulder with the Englishman in many a well-fought field of fame—from Plassy to Goojerat; from the days of Lord Clive to the days of Lord Gough. The feeling of the sepoy is well described in a memorandum which was shown me by a gallant and distinguished officer, which speaks of "his hereditary reverence for the British grenadier, who, though utterly foreign to him in every thought and habit, he regarded habitually as the very impersonation of power in war —'*impiger iracundus*'—inexorable and fierce; not to be handled or approached in time of peace without danger of insult or violence; consuming sacred cattle by herds and intoxicating liquors by the gallon: but all this to be condoned for his lordly bearing in the day of battle, when to storm batteries in the teeth and swarm over intrenchments vainly defended by the flower of India's chivalry was known to be child's play to the dreaded, but, in this respect, honoured British soldier." Such was the native feeling of former days, and this feeling is not likely to be lessened by the heroism with which a handful of Englishmen held India against the power of the mutineers, and vindicated what Macaulay, writing many years earlier, graphically described as "the irresistible energy of the imperial people, the skill against which the bravest troops of Hindostan were helpless as infants, the discipline which had so often triumphed over the frantic struggles of fanaticism and despair, the unconquerable British courage which is never so sedate and stubborn as toward the close of a doubtful and murderous day."

A certain number of native troops being required, the question arose, from what portions of India they could be most advantageously raised. The Madras army was faithful to us in our troubles, and it would have seemed both policy and justice that they should constitute part of the native army which was retained. Nevertheless complaints have been made that regiments which had loyally stood by us in the mutiny were disbanded, and the sepoys insufficiently compensated. Our prestige in India has been greatly due to our scrupulous observance of faith, and it is most undesirable that those soldiers who have been faithful should suffer for the faults of their unfaithful comrades. The Government, however, seems to prefer natives of Northern India, the seat of the mutiny, to those of the South. As regards the hardy tribes who inhabit the vicinity of the mountains which bound India on the north, it is very natural that our military authorities should prefer them. The Sikhs, Pathans, and Goorkhas are among the most warlike of mankind, and an army of such men, led by a Lake or a Wellington, might not unreasonably be expected "to go anywhere and do anything." The military spirit of these men has been described by the poet,—

My father was an Affghan, he came from Candahar,
He rode with Mirza Ameer Khan in the great Mahratta war,
From the Deccan to the Himalay, five hundred of our clan,
They ask'd no leave of king or chief, as they swept through
Hindustan.

They were faithful to us in the mutiny, and their

fidelity enabled Lawrence to make the Punjaub the basis of operations against Delhi. It must, however, be borne in mind that their connexion with us is of comparatively recent date, and that many now living recollect their gallant resistance to the British arms. There is another consideration which may make them less disposed to acquiesce in her Majesty's rule than might have been the case in former days. To such men war is the occupation of their lives. Peace is an ignoble and distasteful waste of life. The great object of England is to maintain, peace, quiet, and order in India, and it may very possibly be that what is our Christian duty and our great merit in the eyes of civilized mankind may appear a great fault in the view of our military retainers. In the present state of the revenue it is most important, wherever it is possible, to contract expenditure, and our military expenditure is the heaviest item in the budget. The number of British regiments cannot be reduced consistently with the safety of our position, and it follows that the only reduction is to be sought in the native army. Our general military policy would seem to be that we should maintain in healthy stations and at points of strategic importance a sufficient number of European troops to suppress any outbreak which may occur, that we should keep for police and other purposes as many native regiments as may be required, and that by a sufficient number of British officers, who should devote themselves to their men and study their habits and feelings, we should endeavour to attach those regiments to our service. What is the policy we pursue? As regards the number of Queen regiments in India probably no complaint can be made, but what is to be deplored is that we maintain a very large, probably a needlessly large, native army, often drawn from those races of our subjects on whom we can least depend, that we arm them with the best rifles, and leave them without the guidance of European officers. We are influenced by the success of Colonel Jacob's celebrated Scinde horse and other distinguished irregular corps, but it must be borne in mind that all men are not Jacobs, Hodsons, and Napiers, and that because a few remarkable men have attained boundless power over the wild natures of the native troops, it does not follow that ordinary mortals will exercise similar influence. The best officers seek employment on the staff corps. It is from this body that the best appointments are filled, and to it aspiring young men look for promotion. Regimental service is too often left to those of inferior ability, and the most absurd stories are told of the deficiencies of the commanders of sepoy battalions. I heard of one case in which a major unable to ride kept his regiment waiting while he walked his horse to the position he had to take. Can we expect that a people who reverence physical superiority will respect such a man? And I was told such cases are not uncommon. The complement of officers professes to be seven, but in many cases it is reduced to three, and these frequently either elderly or invalids. The discipline of the regiments is entrusted to the native officers, to the subahdars and jemadars.

If these were native gentlemen, and if we took this means to attach the old families of India to our rule, there might be much to be said for the system, but I was informed that they were generally soldiers promoted from the ranks, who did not enjoy in any marked degree the confidence and respect of their comrades. Such was the account I heard of the native army from officers I met both in society and in travelling, and the general opinion seemed to be that it was most unsatisfactory. In the event of a regiment being ordered on service, officers from the staff corps are attached to it, but they come new to their men, and the bond of attachment which bound the Company's sepoy to his leader exists no longer.

It is true that the present state of the native army is described as satisfactory by the great authority of Lord Napier of Magdala. I am not aware how far that distinguished general has publicly stated his views, but every one believed that they are not merely the utterances which a high official, placed in a position of great responsibility, is bound to promulgate, but the genuine opinions derived from his large experience. At the same time I was told that he advocates making native gentlemen officers. This would be a great boon if properly carried out. If they were treated as gentlemen bearing her Majesty's commission, on an equality with Englishmen, it would do much to establish our position. What is to be feared is that the snobbism of low-class Englishmen might make their position unpleasant. Lord Napier is probably influenced by his own experience, and his power over the native soldiers is unrivalled. He has served for forty years with them, speaks their languages, knows them well, and trusts them. Whenever we have had first-class officers like him, who have won their confidence by kindness and their admiration by superiority in warlike exercises, we have had no difficulty.

Our course would seem to be to reduce the native army to the number absolutely required, and to take care that those troops are properly and efficiently officered. This would ultimately be a great saving to the Exchequer, though for the present the economy would probably not be felt. It would be necessary to pension the disbanded sepoys, as it is not only right as a matter of justice, but essential as a matter of policy, that they should be treated not only fairly but liberally, while the number of officers would have to be increased. Anything would be better than our present wasteful system, which maintains a large and expensive body of troops which we take no measures to attach to ourselves and to enlist in our interests.

Another subject I heard discussed was the system which keeps the Madras and Bombay armies separate, with separate commanders-in-chief. It is a part, though not an essential part, of the system which maintains distinct governments for Madras and Bombay. The command of these armies is a military question which should be decided by military considerations, though I was told by officers whose prepossessions would be likely to be in favour of the present system, that one commander-in-chief would be sufficient, and that the three armies might with advantage be amalgamated. Probably the Horse Guards are in favour of the present plan, as these appointments give the opportunity of rewarding distinguished officers, a consideration which deserves attention. The army is obviously a greatly underpaid profession, and it is only right that the Duke of Cambridge should wish to retain every means of compensating the pecuniary losses to which military men are subjected. But if great appointments are preserved in India, not for the sake of India, but for the sake of the British army, it follows that the expense should be borne, not by the Indian, but by the Imperial Exchequer. There is far too great a tendency to saddle India with charges which ought to belong to England. Indian finance is not scrutinized by Parliament, and items which might give rise to discussion are too often transferred to it. These remarks suppose that the amalgamation of the three Indian armies might be carried out and an economy thereby effected. If, in the opinion of those competent to form a judgment on military questions, the present system is necessary, of course the charge legitimately falls on the Indian revenue.

CHAPTER VI.

CALCUTTA AND BRITISH POWER IN INDIA.

The distance from Madras to Calcutta is 780 miles, which we accomplished in sixty-nine hours, the shortest run one of the officers of the "Bokhara" said he ever remembered. The sea was very calm, and we were for two days out of sight of land. The P. and O. run their steamers alternate weeks direct from Southampton to Calcutta, communicating at Point de Galle with the China and Australian boats. This is a great convenience to the people of Calcutta, who are thus able to take their families home without a change. The voyage was rather dull, as most of the passengers had left, and there was hardly any one on board. A magnificent swell, attended by a most obsequious native servant, sat next the captain at table, whom I supposed to be a commissioner or some such great man. Judge of my surprise and amusement when I discovered that he was only the pilot who goes to Madras in one ship, and returns to Calcutta in the next, to guide the steamer through the Hooghly. The appointment of pilots to the Hooghly was part of the patronage of the old directors, and this man owed his situation to Sir James Hogg. On getting up on the 22nd, I found we were inside the light-ship at Sandheads, and sailing among buoys, though we could hardly see land. The mud-banks gradually increased till at last we sailed between low banks and found ourselves in the Hooghly, the most western of the mouths by which the Ganges discharges itself into the Bay of Bengal. Mud-banks became gradually converted into low-lying land covered with tropical trees. The scenery is rather interesting, but those who went up the Ganges by sailing-boat in the olden time must have found it very tame. About two we arrived at Garden Reach, where the steamer stopped, near which is the palace of the ex-king of Oude. The domes of Calcutta were imposing from the steamer, and as I drove toward this City of Palaces, the magnificent buildings looked very striking. I took up my quarters at the Great Eastern Hotel, close to Government House, where I spent Sunday. I attended St. John's Church, where I saw a tablet to Daniel Corrie, "first Bishop of Madras, and first Archdeacon of Calcutta, the friend and fellow-labourer of Henry Martyn." As Martyn's life was almost the only book I had with me in my travels, I was particularly interested in this tribute to these holy men. In the afternoon I walked across the Meidan to the cathedral, where are memorials of Bishops Heber and Wilson, the latter of whom is buried there. A native service was going on there. The congregation was small, but it was cause for thankfulness to see service conducted in the great cathedral of Calcutta for a native congregation in a native language by a native clergyman. The cathedral, near which is the Bishop's palace, is situated on one side of the Meidan, a large open space which forms a magnificent park, on the other side of which runs the river, near which Fort William is situated. Fort William, so closely associated with the history of India, is now converted into barracks. Government House overlooks the Meidan, while on the other side, the town extends up the river, on the opposite side of which, Howrah, where is the terminus of the East Indian Railway, is situated. The principal buildings surround Dalhousie Square, a fine space with a garden and a tank in the centre. Statues to Lords Hardinge and Lawrence, and one recently erected to poor Lord Mayo, stand on the Meidan near Government House, Hardinge and Mayo being on horseback. Chouringhee, the fashionable quarter of Calcutta, is on the north side of the Meidan.

On Monday, the 24th, I called on the Viceroy (Lord Northbrook), the Bishop, and Sir Richard Temple, late Finance Minister, and now Lieutenant-Governor of Bengal. On my taking an introduction to the latter from Sir Charles Wingfield, he most kindly invited me to stay with him at Belvedere, where I was hospitably entertained by Lady Temple and himself during the remainder of my stay. Belvedere, the residence of the Governor of Bengal, and originally the villa of Warren Hastings, is situated at Allipore, beyond the Meidan, near Garden Reach, where the steamers land their passengers. I dined with Dr. Milman the Bishop, where I met Mr. Aitcheson, the most distinguished of the Civil Service since the competition system was inaugurated. The Bishop appeared in health, and received his guests with genial hospitality, but it was within two months, and on the day before I reached home, that I heard at Dijon that this excellent prelate had been called to his rest. His death shows the immense importance of that enormous diocese being divided. The early bishops, including the devoted Heber, died in quick succession, but Dr. Wilson held the see for a quarter of a century, and Dr. Cotton died from an accident. On Bishop Wilson's appointment the dioceses of Madras and Bombay were separated, but since that time the Punjaub and other provinces have been added to the empire, and require episcopal supervision. The population of the three dioceses as given me by Mr. Jacob, the Bishop's chaplain, are, Calcutta, 140,000,000; Madras, 40,000,000; Bombay, 20,000,000. Of course these figures comprise the vast Mohammedan and heathen population, but considering that the number of Europeans resident in a district bears a relation to the population, and considering also that the duty of the Church to proclaim the Gospel to these teeming millions, they give some idea of the comparative responsibilities of the three dioceses. Besides, the natives respect us in proportion as they see us in earnest in our own religion. The Bishop told me the native princes had always treated him with great kindness, and on one occasion brought their children to receive his blessing. It is obvious that the work is too great for a single bishop. Two missionary bishops have been conceded to Madras, and it certainly seems right that something should be done to relieve Calcutta of the North-Western part of the see. Bishop Milman has fallen a sacrifice to his labours, and since his death an effort is being made to found a bishopric at Lahore, as a memorial to him. This is a most important object, and good as far as it goes, but it may well be doubted if the diocese of Calcutta will not still remain considerably too large.

On the 25th Sir Richard Temple took me to the Legislative Council of the Governor-General, which is open to the public, though the privilege is not largely availed of, as there were only one other stranger and two reporters present. The question under discussion was a Bill for Coolie emigration into Burmah. It was interesting seeing these great men who rule India, and to whose devotion to the public service we owe so much. The Council Chamber is surrounded by portraits of governors-general and other distinguished statesmen, and here hangs the celebrated portrait of Warren Hastings, immortalized by Macaulay, with "Mens æqua in arduis" above it.

I lunched with Sir Andrew and Lady Clark. Sir Andrew resigned the government of the Straits Settlements to become Minister of Public Works for India, and his removal at a critical moment was one of the causes which led to the Perak complications. It was only natural that he should accept an appointment which presents unequalled attractions to an officer of the Royal Engineers, which is, in fact, the blue riband of his profession; but great blame attaches to the authorities in Downing Street for so regulating their patronage as to lead to such deplorable results. At tiffin I met Captain Bedford, commander of the "Serapis," which was then lying in the river, having brought the Prince from Madras, and Mr. Eden, Commissioner of Burmah. Mr. Eden, who is now one of the most prominent statesmen in India, was honourably distinguished in 1858 for his assertion of the rights of the ryots against the indigo-planters. He decided that when a planter made an advance to a ryot to enable him to grow indigo, and the ryot subsequently declined to grow it, the planter, though he could sue for his money, could not compel the cultivation of the crop. His view of the law is now admitted to be correct, but at the time the indigo-planters were furious. There was a violent controversy, and the then Governor of Bengal made a minute removing Mr. Eden. This, however, was on the eve of his own retirement, and his successor, Sir John Peter Grant, upheld the decision. The question is now settled, and the rights of the ryots are acknowledged, thanks to the firmness of Eden and Grant; but this episode shows the difficulties encountered by the Civil Service in maintaining the rights of the natives against the exactions of mercenary Europeans. One great charge against the East India Company used to be that they discouraged the residence in the country of any Englishmen not in their service. This policy was carried too far; but its justification was, that such emigrants were apt to oppress the ryots, without reference to considerations either of justice or policy. At dinner at Belvedere I met Mr. Bayley, a very old member of the Indian Government.

Next morning Sir Richard showed me a memorandum on the finances of India, in reply to Fawcett's great speech of 1872, at which time he was Finance Minister. Virtually it was a great tribute to the ability of Fawcett's speech. A member of Parliament who has never resided in India, whatever his talent and whatever his industry, is sure to fall into error; but when the Professor's statements come to be examined by the greatest statesmen in India, the errors turn out to be trifling. In the afternoon he took me to a party at Sir William Muir's, formerly Governor of the North-West Provinces, and now Finance Minister, where we met Mr. Hobhouse, the legal member of Council, and Sir Richard Meade, lately on the Baroda Commission, and now about to proceed as Resident to Hyderabad. I should think he would have a difficult task before him, as Lord Northbrook's behaviour to Sir Salar Jung in doubting his statement that the health of the Nizam prevented his meeting the Prince of Wales was wanting in courtesy to that distinguished native statesman, and calculated to sow the seeds of future trouble in that part of the country. At Hyderabad, as at Baroda, Lord Northbrook sows the wind and leaves Lord Lytton to reap the whirlwind. Many of the politicians of Calcutta advocate the abolition of the separate governments of

Madras, and more particularly of Bombay, and the reduction of the rulers of these Presidencies to the rank of Lieutenant-Governors. The Lieutenant-Governor virtually exercises the same civil power as a Governor, but he has no control over the army, and is responsible to the Viceroy, while the Governors of Madras and Bombay correspond direct with the Secretary of State. The question is one of much importance, but it is one on which it is difficult for any one who has not been behind the scenes either in India or in Downing Street to form an opinion. It is said that the independent jurisdiction of the Governor of Bombay (I was informed by high authority that the Government of Madras had always been very loyal to that of Calcutta) led to conflicting measures being taken and to serious inconvenience. On the other hand, the people of Bombay, both official and private, are jealous of the capital. Probably the wonderful progress of the western city of recent years has led its inhabitants to aspire to the first position in India, and, at all events, to be anxious to retain the privileges of a separate Government, with a Governor and Council. The suggested change would no doubt be economical; but there is one consideration that should not be lost sight of, and which is, that if Lieutenant-Governors were substituted for Governors, English statesmen would cease to take part in affairs in India except in the character of Viceroys. It tends to keeping up the ties between the two countries that English statesmen of first-class rank should occasionally go out to India, and it becomes us to hesitate before we alter a system which insures such a result. It is a great advantage to have an appointment which the Duke of Buckingham, an ex-Secretary of State, is willing to accept; and though ill-health has prematurely closed the public career of the late Governor of Bombay, Sir Seymour Fitzgerald, yet, if we look back to the Parliament of 1859, we shall recollect that, next to the present Premier and the present Lord Chancellor, he was the most prominent member of the Conservative party, and the question of his holding high Cabinet rank seemed to be simply the question of Lord Derby returning to power. A system which secures such men for India should not be altered on light grounds. I dined at a large party at Government House, where the rooms are very splendid.

Early next morning the Governor, who has been most kind in showing me "the Capital of Asia," of which he is naturally very proud, took me a ride to the bridge not long since constructed across the Hooghly. We passed the site of the Black Hole, where that horrid crime was perpetrated which ultimately led to the subjugation of Bengal by the English, of which no vestige remains. The wharves which have been constructed along the banks of the river are very striking, and do great credit to the Bengal Government. They are crowded with large ocean-going steamers, which, since the opening of the canal, carry on the commerce between Great Britain and India. To make these wharves many of the ghauts down which the people go to bathe in the sacred

Ganges had to be moved. The Hindoos, however, seem to be very reasonable, and so long as accommodation is provided for them to perform their ablutions, they do not object to alterations. The buildings of Calcutta are very splendid, and the administration of each succeeding Governor of Bengal is distinguished by some improvement. The University is a fine building, and the hospitals seem well managed. The medical schools, both of Calcutta and Madras, seem to be doing a very useful work in educating natives to the practice of the profession.

Mr. Colvin, private secretary to Sir Louis Malet, was stopping at Belvedere. Sir Louis Malet was staying at Government House, and was understood to have come out about some question between the English and the Indian Government. Rumour said the English Government wanted to reimpose the income-tax; but when I reached Bombay the matter was explained by the publication of the correspondence between Lord Salisbury and Lord Northbrook about the duty on Manchester goods, Sir Louis Malet at this time was ill and unable to attend to business, and had shortly afterwards to return home. Another gentleman I met at Belvedere was Mr. Metcalfe, nephew of the great Lord Metcalfe, who had come to Calcutta in consequence of an apprehended scarcity of food, and who had been actively engaged in the relief of the famine of 1873-4. In regard to that famine, the Indian Government—particularly the Viceroy, Sir George Campbell, and Sir Richard Temple—have been blamed that their measures for its relief were not sufficiently influenced by considerations of economy; that more money was spent than turned out to be necessary. To my mind this is the highest praise that can be awarded them. Economy is everywhere and always an admirable thing, and in India, in the critical state of the revenue, it is an indispensable virtue; but when famine threatens, when the lives of millions are at stake, it must give way to the urgent necessity of saving human life. With the difficulties which have to be encountered in India from deficiency of communication, it was the imperative duty of the Government to provide on the largest scale for the most unfavourable contingencies. What would have been said if too little provision had been made, and if a large sacrifice of life had been the consequence? If the Viceroy erred at all, he erred on the right side, and his error does him honour. This is evident when we consider the fearful history of previous similar visitations. Whatever the faults of Lord Northbrook's administration, his conduct during the famine deserves the gratitude both of the country he represented and of the country which he ruled.

In the afternoon Lady Temple had a garden party, where I met Sir William Muir, Sir Richard Meade, Sir Douglas Forsyth, Sir Richard Garth, late M.P. for Guildford, and now Chief Justice of India, and several natives of distinction, including Rajah Narendra Krisna, a member of the Viceroy's Council, and Baboo Krisdas Pal, a member of that of the Lieutenant-Governor of Bengal. With both these gentlemen I had an interesting conversation. Rajah Narendra Krisna is a Brahmin by caste, and a large zemindar. To my surprise he seemed utterly ignorant of the ryotwaree system of Madras, and unable to comprehend how any province could go on without a permanent settlement. These wealthy zemindars are much opposed to the income-tax. On Krislodas Pal I had previously called with a letter of introduction. He is the editor of the *Hindoo Patriot*, a man of great ability, and intellectually the leader of Hindoo public opinion. He was kind enough to give me a large number of pamphlets on public questions, from which I learned his views. He warmly advocates the English education of the natives, and urges many reforms which I think might with advantage be granted. At the same time it struck me that he is to be regarded rather as the representative of the zemindars than of the natives generally. The rich zemindars, under Lord Cornwallis's permanent settlement, have become the proprietors of the land of Bengal. From their wealth and their intelligence they must always have influence; but it is to be borne in mind that beneath them are the vast body of ryots, often living in the greatest poverty, and with little or no means of making their feelings and their grievances known.

I dined with Sir Alexander Arbuthnot, the Madras member of the Viceroy's Council, where I met Mr. Bayley, Mr. Metcalfe, Mr. Colvin, and Colonel Earle, Military Secretary to Lord Northbrook. We afterwards went to a party given by Captain Bedford and the officers of the "Serapis," where was a performance of Christy Minstrels, which ended with a dance. The "Serapis" lay moored along the banks of the river, and as we left, the blue lights she burned were very pretty.

The 28th was my last day at Calcutta, so I went to the Oriental Bank to get money for my journey. The governments of the three Presidencies issue notes for sums of from five rupees upwards. The notes of one Presidency are not payable in another, and I was told a discount is sometimes charged on them, though I never found this the case myself. Although the rupee has been very much more depressed since my visit, the depreciation at this time was becoming serious. To a traveller, of course, it was a gain, as in the present instance I saved thirteen per cent. by it; but to that large body of residents in the East, who have to make heavy remittances home for the maintenance and education of their children, the loss was frightful. The idea suggests itself whether a gold could not be substituted for a silver coinage; but I was assured by those of whom I asked the question, that the native habit of turning gold coins into ornaments would present a great impediment. I called to take leave of Sir W. Muir, who very kindly gave me letters to Benares, Agra, and Roorkee, where he recommended me to visit the Ganges Canal. He is a most interesting and superior man—one of those statesmen who have done so much to consolidate the British Empire in the East. I also called to take leave of the poor bishop, whom I then hoped shortly to see again, as he was contemplating a hurried trip to England. In the afternoon I accompanied Sir R. Temple to a meeting, over which he presided, for establishing a school for technical education in commemoration of the Prince's visit. I was much interested in being present, as, with the exception of the Governor and his aide-de-camp, the assembly was entirely composed of natives, who made speeches, often able and eloquent, in English. The discussion was warm, some advocating a high-class institution, and others one of a more general and practical character. At last the parties seemed so hopelessly divided, that the only solution appeared to be for each to pursue its own plan, and found its own institution. On our return we visited the native hospital, and passed the Martiniere; a great orphan asylum. After dinner I took leave of my kind friends, who were going to a ball at Government House, and proceeded to the Howrah station of the East Indian Railway on the other side of the Hooghly, where I took the train for Benares. Sir Richard and Lady Temple had been unceasing in their kindness, and I felt it a great advantage to be in the society of the greatest Indian statesman of the present day, whose knowledge of everything connected with the country is probably unrivalled. The object of my journey was to increase my knowledge of a country in which I had long taken an interest, and of which, having been a member of the Committee of the last Parliament on East Indian Finance, I had heard much. This may be a convenient place for somo general observations on the information I received.

The original connexion of England with India was commercial. The East India Company went to India to trade, and did not become political till circumstances forced greatness upon it. The genius of Clive and Hastings conquered an empire, when their masters, the merchant princes of Leadenhall-street, would have preferred a less ambitious policy. The importance of the territory thus acquired forced itself on public attention; the eloquence of Burke urged the claims of the people of India for just government, and the result was the system established by Pitt, which continued in force for more than seventy years. By this system the administration was carried on in the name of the Company, but the political acts of the Company were submitted to the Board of Control, which consisted of the Ministers of the Crown, and which was, of course, responsible to Parliament. In 1814 the Company was precluded from trading in India, and in 1834 their trade to China was prohibited, and they were confined to their functions as a governing body. They consisted of the Court of Proprietors, composed of those who held 1000*l*. of their stock, who met quarterly, debated Indian questions, and elected a Court of twenty-four directors, in whom the power was lodged. This Court administered the government, subject to the supervision of the Board of Control, which had a veto on their proceedings, and on political questions had the power of overruling their wishes by sending out orders, often contrary to their views, through what was called the Secret Committee. It was in this way that Sir John Cam Hobhouse, in defiance of the opinion of the directors, ordered the army to cross the Sutlej, and forced on the Affghan war.

One of the most important functions of the directors was patronage. It was felt in 1783, and continued to be felt in 1858, that to place the vast patronage of the East in the hands of the minister of the day would be fraught with danger to the very existence of the British Constitution. Hence it was left in the hands of the Company, and, when that venerable body ceased to exist, was disposed of by competitive examination. The directors were, for the most part, gentlemen who had distinguished themselves in India. It was the natural and laudable ambition of those who had spent their lives with distinction in the service of the Company, on their return home, to become members of the governing body. The great objection to the system was, that as many of the proprietors knew nothing of India, and cared for nothing but their dividends, some of the most distinguished statesmen declined to submit to the humiliation of a personal canvass. But, despite this disadvantage, the Court always contained a large amount of Indian experience. It had the advantage of keeping the conduct of Eastern affairs in the hands of men trained from their earliest years in the traditions of the service. The most distinguished Indian statesman has no power, under the present plan of competition, of placing his son in the service. Formerly he was able to do so as a matter of course. Directors occasionally prostituted their patronage to jobbery, but, nevertheless, many of them honourably disposed of it to the children of those who had claims on the Company. A director would say, "I recollect So-and-so rendering great services in Orissa twenty years ago, and I will give his son a writership." The young man so appointed had a basis of knowledge which it takes his successor selected by competition many years to acquire. He had been born in India, and his infant lips had lisped in Bengalee or Tamil. The conversation at his father's table had been on Indian questions, and he landed in Hindustan with an acquaintance with the country such as cannot be possessed by one who has no hereditary connexion with it. Previous to leaving England he was sent to Haileybury, where those nominated to writerships were grounded in Oriental studies. Haileybury had this great advantage, that it threw the future rulers of India together in close personal intercourse, and gave them that intimate knowledge of each other's abilities and characters which can only be acquired in schools and colleges. A man's talents were appreciated before he arrived, his reputation had preceded him, and the acquaintance of the service with each other was of great advantage. It was true that many incompetent men were nominated by the favouritism of corrupt directors, but when they arrived they were relegated to positions where their incompetence was not likely to be felt, while the better class of directors took a pride in the achievements of their nominees. Now there is no *esprit de corps* in the service. A Civil Servant lands, knowing nothing of his colleagues, and has to acquire much which was intuitive to his predecessor. It is said that "many of the Company's men were failures, but others had genius The Queen has fewer failures, but also fewer men of genius." It must be borne in mind that we do not yet see the full effect of the change which was inaugurated in 1854. The great men who now rule the East were appointed by the directors. The Temples, the Muirs, the Stracheys, the Meades, and the Huddlestones, were all originally in the Company's service. It will not be for some ten or twelve years to come, when the last of John Company's servants shall have retired to an honourable and well-earned repose at home, that we shall appreciate the full importance of the alteration which deprived India of the hereditary knowledge insured by the old system.

It would appear that many of the advantages possessed by the institution at Haileybury might be again secured by placing those who have passed the examination for an appointment in a college to commence together their Oriental studies. It is much to be regretted that Lord Salisbury should have decided against this scheme, which would at least have brought the service into communication and acquaintance with each other. A yet more important question is, "Can nothing be done to enable the sons of those who have served their country in the East to follow the career in which their fathers have been honourably distinguished?"

The son of an old Indian can offer qualifications for the service of his Sovereign which others do not possess. He has facilities for acquiring a knowledge of the habits, the feelings, and the languages of the natives. He enjoys their respect, in many instances their affection, in a way not vouchsafed to any man who comes fresh to the country. On the other hand, it is only justice to those who devote their lives to the service of England in a trying climate, that their children should be placed in an advantageous position for succeeding them as compared with those who have no such claim. The army in India is much better paid than it is at home, while the Civil Service is the most highly remunerated under the Crown; but, taking all this into account, her Majesty's Indian servants deserve every consideration. Though their salaries are liberal, the cost of living in India is great, and they are involved in great expense from the necessity of educating their children at home. All that an Indian can expect to do with the utmost prudence is to realize a moderate competency on which to spend his declining years in England. Such men deserve every consideration at the hands of their country. The case might be met without any violent alteration of the present system. All nominations might continue to be given by competition, but it might be enacted that half of them should be reserved for the sons of those who had spent twenty years either in the military or civil service of the Crown in India. Such a change would be a boon to a most deserving body of men—a body of men to whom their Sovereign and country are deeply indebted—and it would secure for the East the services of those whose acquaintance with the country dated from their earliest years and associations.

Although destitute of power, the Court of Proprietors had its use in enlightening public opinion on Oriental questions. Men who had spent their lives in administering the affairs of the East always found a difficulty in entering the House of Commons—a difficulty which has been much increased by each succeeding Reform Bill. The Court of Proprietors afforded an arena whose custom secured a report of their speeches, and where they were able to give the public the benefit of their enlarged experience. The great Company has passed into history, and many faults may be laid to its charge. The Christian must deeply deplore that the directors did not appreciate the responsibility of giving every facility for the spread of the Gospel. It is of course a duty to grant the fullest amount of toleration, and even to permit some things which would not be allowed in a Christian country; but, at the same time, it is a duty to afford to missionaries every opportunity of proclaiming the unsearchable riches of Christ to the population around them. They have been charged with carrying on unjust and unnecessary wars of aggression, though, as regards these, they for the most part acted under the orders of the Board of Control. The production of opium and the salt-tax had their origin under their *régime*. On the other hand, we can but admire the genius and the energy which converted a few trading factories into a magnificent empire, and which governed teeming millions in peace, and on the whole in prosperity. The proud boast of the petition[1] in which the Company, opposing their extinction in 1858, addressed Parliament was fully justified :—" If the character of the East India Company alone were concerned, your petitioners would be willing to await the verdict of history. They are satisfied that posterity will do them justice." But whatever the merits of the Company, they were at that moment discredited by the want of foresight which preceded the mutiny, and their numerous enemies took advantage of the crisis to secure their fall. The Government of India was transferred to the Crown, it being fondly supposed that, when the House of Commons was in name as well as in fact the paramount power, it would give increased attention to Eastern affairs. At that time the great apprehension entertained by the opponents of the change, and especially by their illustrious leader, Mr. Thomas Baring, was that India would become " the shuttlecock of party." Whatever the danger may have been, the disastrous collapse of Mr. Cardwell's motion on the Talookdars of Oude seems to have taught the House that Indian subjects were not adapted for party conflicts. The large-acred squires and the rich merchants and manufacturers, who comprise so large a proportion of the assembly,

[1] This petition, which contained an able and exhaustive defence of the administration of the Company, was the composition of two very eminent men, Sir James Melvill and Mr. John Stuart Mill.

know nothing of India, and, when an Indian subject is debated, are conspicuous by their absence. The result is that India is less known to the British public then when its affairs were ventilated in the Court of Proprietors. When Mr. Grant Duff brought in his first Budget in 1869, Colonel Sykes paid him the curious compliment of informing him that "he was the first Indian Minister he recollected who could get forty members to listen to him." A few members, notably Professor Fawcett, have felt their responsibility to the people of India, but as a rule the House of Commons has been scandalously indifferent to Indian subjects. The Indian Council is supposed to take the place of the Court of Directors in administering the finances, and Mr. Gladstone once informed the House that to pass a resolution about opium would be to interfere with their functions. No doubt the advice and assistance of a body of experienced Indian statesmen is valuable to the Secretary of State, but their constitution precludes their exercising any control over him.

Every one who pays any attention to Indian questions must be aware that finance is the great difficulty we have to encounter. We have an inelastic revenue, a constantly increasing expenditure, and our embarrassments have lately been augmented by the fall in the value of silver. The chief items of revenue are:—

Land	£21,000,000
Opium	8,400,000 [2]

[2] This is the gross revenue. Some £2,000,000 has to be deducted for expenses.

Salt	£6,200,000
Stamps	2,800,000
Customs	2,600,000
Excise	2,500,000
Tributes	700,000
Irrigation and State Railways	1,000,000
Miscellaneous, Receipts, Army, Post Office, Telegraphs, &c.	5,300,000
Total	£50,500,000

The land revenue is the principal item of receipts, and has not of late years shown much elasticity:—

In 1869-70 it amounted to	£21,066,929
„ 1870-71 „ „ „	20,622,823
„ 1871-72 „ „ „	20,520,337
„ 1872-73 „ „ „	21,348,669
„ 1873-74 „ „ „	21,037,912
„ 1874-75 „ „ „	21,296,793

The revised estimate for 1875-76 and the Budget estimate for 1876-77 are about the same.

It is evident that the land revenue cannot be looked to for any increase, and, so far as I could gather, it was already at a figure which presses with undue severity on the inhabitants of many districts. It is raised differently in different provinces, but the main systems are the zemindaree, where the tax is paid by the zemindar or native proprietor; the ryotwaree, where it is collected from the ryot or cultivator direct; and the village, where a small community organize themselves into a kind of municipality, and the head men of this community apportion the payments, and hand the proceeds to the collector. In Bengal much of the land is held under Lord Cornwallis's Permanent Settlement of 1793. That Settlement is generally held to have been a great mistake. It guaranteed the zemindar, who had collected it for former native princes, against any increase of assessment, thus converting the tax-collectors into proprietors, and it did so at a time when, as was pointed out by Sir John Shore (afterwards Lord Teignmouth and Governor-General), owing to a great recent famine, the assessment was unusually low. But, whatever the mistake at the time, the faith of the country is pledged to its permanence, and the zemindars, who from a kind of middle-men were converted into landed proprietors, are entitled to reap the advantages conceded to them by Lord Cornwallis. But while every idea of interfering with their rights ought to be repudiated and denounced, it cannot be admitted that the Permanent Settlement should exempt them from income-tax, should that tax ever be generally imposed. The misfortune of the Permanent Settlement is that it precludes the State from taking advantage of any rise in the value of land; and as no increase of revenue is possible from the rich provinces of Bengal, the necessities of the Exchequer press with undue severity on the landed interest in other parts of India. At the same time it undoubtedly promotes the wealth of the settled districts, and enables the Government to collect the revenue with ease. Sir R. Temple, in his "Report on the Administration of Bengal for 1874-75," says on this point, "As might be well expected under the Permanent Settlement, the ordinary land revenue is collected with such ease and punctuality that nothing is left for remark or narrative."

Of the twenty-one millions of land revenue, three and a half are under the Permanent Settlement. The remainder is obtained by other plans. The common system in the North seems to be a settlement for thirty years, which, at the end of that period, is liable to alteration. This seems fair, both for the Government and the proprietor, but unfortunately the tax is fixed at so high a rate as to weigh with undue severity. Take the case of the Talookdars of Oude, of whom we heard so much at the time of Mr. Cardwell's attack on Lord Derby on this question in 1858. The Talookdars are the landowners of Oude, subject to a rent of fifty per cent. for land-tax, and five per cent. for local charges. This charge seems enormous, though it is said to be so assessed as not to come to so much. In Madras the land revenue "is fixed on each field, to be paid *for good crops;* if the crop fail, the revenue is reduced, and there is an annual settlement on cultivated land."[3] Such a system gives little inducement for the improvement of agriculture, and we can hardly wonder if we hear of land being thrown out of cultivation. Under these circumstances we cannot look for much increase of the land revenue, and it might well be wished that our finances were in a condition which would permit of its pressure being lightened. Some remarks of the Duke of Argyll, in a despatch of May

[3] Blue Book on East India Progress, 1872-73, p. 26.

22nd, 1873, deserve attentive consideration :—"I observe, with much satisfaction, that the Lieutenant-Governor in his minute discourages the notion that whatever is gained by the owner of land, in the shape of rent, is so much lost to the State. The best wealth of a Government is to be found in the growing wealth of its people; and the feeling which leads it to grudge all that does not fall into the hands of its tax collector is a very short-sighted feeling, and must lead, if really followed, to a very short-sighted policy. . . . . . Under the system of land revenue which has long prevailed in India, the proportion of the total produce of the soil which is absorbed by the State is very large. Proprietors of the smaller class who do not enjoy more, and who generally enjoy less than one-half the rental, are not in the position which enables the proprietors of land in other countries to expend largely out of their incomes upon the permanent improvement of the soil. . . . . . When the Government appropriates a large proportion of that surplus produce of the soil, which in all countries must be the foundation of individual and national wealth, it cannot expect the people to have the enterprising and independent spirit which that wealth promotes."

Opium is the next great item in the Budget, and the revenue derived from it resolves itself into two heads: the profit realized by its cultivation and sale at Calcutta, and the transit duly levied by the Bombay Government on its passage through their territories. The system under which the first portion is collected is described by Sir Cecil Beadon, late Lieutenant-Governor of Bengal, in his evidence before the Committee of the House of Commons. He stated that "the existing mode of raising the revenue had been in force almost ever since the commencement of our rule in Bengal, and had been gradually growing for a number of years;" that "the Government has established two agencies, one at Patna, and the other at Ghazeepore, which are usually called the Behar agency and the Benares agency; the head-quarters of the one being at Patna, and of the other at Ghazeepore;" that "when any ryot wishes to cultivate opium, he goes to the sub-agent, and asks to have his name registered, his land measured, and to get a cultivation licence, and the usual advance. The sub-agent makes inquiries—ascertains that the man is really *bona fide* an owner of the land which he proposes to cultivate with opium, has the land measured, and then makes the advance upon the security of the person himself, to whom the advance is made, and his fellow-villagers. The advance is made shortly before the sowing season. The ryot then sows his land, and when the plant is above ground, the land is then measured by one of the native establishments, and if the ryot has sown all that he engaged to sow, he gets a second advance; if he has not sown so much, he gets something less in proportion, or if more he gets a little more. This is a sort of rough settlement of the second advance. Nothing further takes place till the crop is ripe for gathering, and when the ryot has gathered the crop he collects it in vessels, and takes it to the sub-agent's office; there he delivers it to the sub-agent, as the agent of the Government, and receives the full price for it, subject to further adjustment, when the opium has been weighed and tested, and examined at the agent's factory. The opium is then collected at the sub-agency and forwarded to the factory; there it is exposed for a considerable time in large masonry tanks; it is reduced to a uniform consistency, and made fit for the market, some for home consumption, and some for sale in Calcutta for exportation—the greater quantity for exportation. It is then packed in cases and sent to Calcutta, and in Calcutta it is sold by auction at periodical sales, and exported by merchants for consumption abroad." That "the extent of land so cultivated is limited according to the financial needs of the Government; it is limited entirely upon Imperial considerations. The Government of India, theoretically at least, if not practically, decide how much opium they will bring to market; and, of course, upon that depends the quantity of land they will put under cultivation, and make advances for." That "it is absolutely prohibited for any one to cultivate opium without a licence," and that "there is no illicit cultivation at all."

Such is the system as detailed on the high authority of Sir Cecil Beadon; and no one can pretend, after reading his statement, that our connexion with opium is simply a parallel case to the duty we levy on spirits at home. As regards spirits, our legislation, though it might be carried farther, is a legislation of repression. We impose a heavy duty, and we enact that the sale shall not take place except in houses licensed by the authority of the State. We might raise the duty, and we might prohibit the sale; but if, on the other hand, we did away with the duty, and permitted the sale without licence, we should immensely increase the consumption. Chancellors of the Exchequer may find an increased consumption a help to their Budget, but the action of the British Parliament has been to throw impediments in the way of drinking. Contrast this with the action of the Indian Government in regard to opium. When a deficiency of revenue is feared, the Council of the Viceroy urge that "the most energetic steps should be taken to increase the production."[4] They "only regard opium as a means of revenue."[5] They discourage, it is true, the consumption of the drug among their own subjects, but when it is a question of revenue on the one hand, or of poisoning thousands of unhappy Chinese on the other, they regard the demoralization and extinction of a friendly nation with perfect indifference. They do not view opium, as a British statesman views spirits, as an article whose consumption is to be discouraged. They view it rather as a distiller, and consider that money is to be made without reference to moral considerations. The position of the Indian Government in regard to opium is not analogous to that of the British

[4] Minute of Sir J. Strachey, September 20, 1869.

[5] Sir C. Beadon's answer to Mr. Fawcett. Question 3329.

Chancellor of the Exchequer who taxes spirits, but rather to that of the distiller who produces them. We may be told that we are simply supplying the Chinese with a soothing and a harmless luxury. Such was not the opinion of the East India Company. The Court of Directors, in a memorable despatch, condemned opium in perhaps the tersest and most powerful sentence which has ever been written on the subject:—"*Were it possible to put an end to the use of the drug altogether, except for medical purposes, we would gladly do it in compassion to mankind.*" And yet, under the administration of the Company, the exportation of opium, which, in the time of Warren Hastings, began with some 200 chests, grew to over 70,000. With a great admiration for the Company, whose faults seem to me to have been exaggerated, and whose merits to have been very insufficiently appreciated, I cannot but feel that the way in which, under the sanction and with the support of the Home Government, they taught the Chinese the taste for this deleterious drug, is the great blot in their escutcheon.

The Company fell, and the disgust felt throughout the length and breadth of the land, when attention was called to this question in 1857, by General Alexander, Joseph Sturge, (the late eminent philanthropist) and others, was one element which led to their fall, but the Government which succeeded them have intensified and perpetuated the evil. The responsibility of the Company was assumed by the British nation, and I cannot but fear that for our conduct on this subject we have to give a solemn account. The question was first brought before Parliament in the time of the Company, in the year 1843, when Lord Ashley (the present Earl of Shaftesbury) moved a resolution to the effect that the trade with China "was damaging to our legitimate commerce, and utterly inconsistent with the honour and duty of a great Christian country." This motion was withdrawn on Sir Robert Peel's stating that delicate negotiations were going on with China, with which it would be inconvenient to interfere. Though a good deal of public attention was called to this question in 1856 and 1857, the dissolution of the latter year prevented its being brought before Parliament. I am not aware that it was ever alluded to in the House till the Indian Budget of 1869, when I ventured to say a few words upon it, stating that "I had always regarded the conduct of this country in forcing this poisonous and deleterious drug upon the Chinese as the greatest blot on the name of the British nation."

The following year Sir Wilfrid Lawson moved that "this House condemns the system by which a large portion of the Indian revenue is raised from opium." This motion was defeated on a division, after Mr. Gladstone had lectured the House on interfering with a matter which belonged to the Indian Council. In 1875 Mr. Mark Stewart moved that "this House is of opinion that the Imperial policy regulating the opium traffic between India and China should be carefully considered by her Majesty's Government, with a view to the gradual withdrawal of the Government of India from the cultivation and manufacture of opium." This resolution was also defeated.

It will be seen that the House of Commons has three times sanctioned the present system—once during the *régime* of the Company, and twice in recent years.

Whatever the guilt incurred by the Company, it has clearly been assumed by Parliament. It is a sad consideration that the evil has grown to such a point that it seems most difficult to find a way of escape. In 1843 the revenue in question was only 2,000,000*l.*; now it has swollen to 6,000,000*l.* Had Lord Shaftesbury succeeded, the revenue would long ere this have been replaced from other sources; and as the Chinese Government were sincerely desirous to suppress the use of opium, this fearful vice would have been uncommon, if not unknown, in China. Now the Chinese have become so accustomed to the indulgence, and their Government is so powerless, that it is to be feared that nothing that we can do will stop the consumption. It is also to be feared that it is perfectly true, as alleged by the advocates of opium, that the Chinese will have it, and that if we do not supply it they will procure it elsewhere. India has become increasingly dependent on this revenue, and though it may be urged that the increased and increasing cultivation in China makes this revenue most precarious, it is replied that present necessities leave no room for considerations of future danger. The situation illustrates the well-known lines of the poet,—

> "Facilis descensus Averni;
> Noctes atque dies patet atri janua Ditis;
> Sed revocare gradum, superasque evadere ad auras,
> Hoc opus, hic labor est."

When in Parliament I spoke strongly on this question, but I always felt that it is one for the people of England, and that if they wish to get rid of the responsibility they must be prepared for a sacrifice similar to that which they made for the abolition of slavery. The people of England are trustees for the people of India. Under their administration—with the sanction of their representatives—this system has grown up, and they have no right to tax their subjects to make up for their own errors. It would be impossible, without gross oppression, to raise the taxation of India by 6,000,000*l*. If, therefore, we wish to relieve ourselves from the responsibility of this reproach to the British name, we must be prepared to put our hands in our own pockets. We must not oppress the Hindoos to atone for our own faults, and, unless we are prepared for a great sacrifice, I see no remedy for this evil. Parliament, of course, could not legislate unless the state of public feeling was very different to that which now exists, and the subject must be left to the consciences of the British people.[6]

Many persons who will not be prepared to agree

[6] I need hardly point out that a middle course might be pursued by a Government earnestly anxious to abate this great evil. They might at once arrest the increased cultivation of the poppy, with a view gradually to diminish the supply and to substitute for opium other sources of revenue.

with me in the strong views which I have expressed will think that the Bengal system, to which I have hitherto referred, might be advantageously abandoned. A great portion of the opium produced is not grown under our rule, but is cultivated in the native States, particularly in the territories of Holkar. This opium, which passes under the name of Malwa opium, pays a duty of 600 rupees per chest for transit through the British territory, and is shipped from Bombay. It has been gradually increasing, till in the years 1872-73 and 1873-74 the Malwa opium exceeded the Bengal. The fact of so large a proportion being produced by native States would now constitute an additional difficulty in suppressing the traffic. It will be seen that, as regards this opium, the analogy which is attempted to be drawn between the Indian revenue from opium and the British revenue from spirits is much more applicable, and it has been proposed to assimilate the Bengal system to the Bombay, by giving up the Government advances to the ryot for cultivation, and by levying an export duty.

The great advocate of this change is Sir William Muir, who, when Governor of the North-West Provinces, explained his views in a very able Minute, dated February 22, 1868. This document begins with a discussion of the Bombay pass duty, which, having been at first 175 rupees per chest, and afterwards as low as 125, has been gradually raised, till, in 1861, it stood at 700 and since 1862 has remained at 600. The distinguished author seems to incline to the opinion that the state of the market would permit the duty to be raised to 700 or even 800 rupees per chest without injury to the trade. He then proceeds to advocate "superseding the singular, and, to my mind, objectionable arrangement, under which the Bengal Government monopolizes the growth, manufacture, and sale of the drug." He goes on to say, "I am not insensible to the difficulties surrounding this question. Besides all other risks to the revenue, there is the danger of smuggling. This already exists to some considerable degree. But if free or licensed cultivation be allowed in Malwa and Bombay without any practical risk of evasion along its extensive sea-board, I cannot see what greater risk there could be in Bengal. The growth of the poppy might still remain prohibited on this side Behar, and further security might be obtained by making the cultivation subject to licence, as suggested by the Allahabad Board and Sir R. Hamilton." He then proceeds to argue that a duty of 700 rupees per chest all round would yield close on to six millions sterling, which is equivalent to, or even more, than the present net revenue, and that the Government, by a uniform duty, would probably have the Chinese market far more under its command than by the present double system. He calls attention to the expensive nature of the present plan, the cost of a chest to the Government averaging 300 rupees, and having risen in 1861-2 to 420. He also alludes to "the inconveniences and loss to the Government from the locking up of enormous sums distributed in advance to the cultivators." According to Sir Charles Trevelyan, "the greater part of the advances of two years must always be outstanding," and in 1864 the amount thus lent out was estimated at two millions and three-quarters sterling, on which large amount no interest was charged. After considering several questions of detail, such as licences for cultivation, smuggling, and the steps which would be required to make the alterations, Sir William Muir concludes,—"Surely a case has been made out to justify at the least inquiry. *Prima facie*, the change proposed would remove a blemish from the administration without imperilling the finances. That cannot be an edifying position for the Government to occupy, in which it has year by year to determine the quantity of opium it will bring to sale, and in which there is a constant inducement for it to trim the market, and in which its haste to secure wider harvests and larger returns has repeatedly recoiled upon the trade, stimulated baneful speculation and gambling in Central and Western India, and ended in much misery. I do not speak of the undignified aspect of the British Government growing, manufacturing, and selling the drug—performing, in fact, all the functions of producer and speculator. I will merely ask what the impression is on the mind when we see Holkar performing the functions of opium-trader, which are now discharged by the Government of Bengal."

"The change would relieve the British Government from the odious imputation of pandering to the vice of China by overstimulating production, overstocking the market, and flooding China with the drug, in order to raise a wider and more secure revenue to itself—an imputation of which at least on one occasion I fear we are not wholly guiltless. A few years ago, when the Government of Bengal was straining every nerve to extend the cultivation of the poppy, I was witness to the discontent of the agricultural population of certain districts west of the Jumna, from which the crop was for the first time being raised. Where the system of advances has long been in vogue, and the mode of preparing the drug is well understood, no doubt the poppy is a popular crop ; though even there the system of Government monopoly gives to Government officers a power of interference over those who have once taken their advances, which must be liable to abuse. But the case to which I allude is that of new districts where the poppy had not hitherto been grown, and into which the Bengal Board were endeavouring to extend the cultivation by the bait of large advances among an unwilling peasantry, and at the risk of innoculating them with a taste for a deleterious drug; and all this with the sole view of securing a wider area of poppy cultivation, and thus a firmer grasp of the China market." "The impropriety of the position was to my mind painful." "By retiring from the monopoly the Government of India will avoid these and all other unseemly imputations. China wants opium: our traders and merchants are ready to supply it. The licence duty will still support the revenue, and thus the action of the Government will be that of check, and no longer of stimulus. The fluctuations in the demands of China will be met in the ordinary course of trade, by corresponding variations in the supply from India. The area of cultivation will be adjusted by the direct action of the Chinese themselves upon speculators and producers, and will no longer depend upon the arbitrary will of the Government. To bring about results so desirable in themselves, and so closely affecting the good name of the British Government, is surely a sufficient warrant for the appointment of a Commission."

I have troubled my readers with these long quotations because it seems to me they deserve the attentive consideration of every one who can exert any influence over Eastern affairs. These are no Utopian sentiments. They are not the sentiments of a missionary who reprobates the trade on account of the evil it causes to the Chinese. They are not the sentiments of a student who has gained his acquaintance with Indian affairs from the perusal of reports and blue books at home. They are the sentiments of a great statesman, who has filled the highest offices in India, through a career of unusual length, with extraordinary distinction and success. The views of such a man cannot be dismissed as Utopian and impracticable; and though the change he advocates cannot atone for the past, cannot even lessen the demoralization which is now injuring the Chinese, his plan would at least place England in a less objectionable position.

I had always understood that the British Government endeavoured to discourage the consumption of opium among our own subjects. On this point I did not obtain much definite information; but my general impression is that it is to be feared that the use of opium is increasing in India. I heard on high authority that its consumption increases in Burmah, though it is heavily taxed. It must be difficult, if not impossible for the Government, connected as they are with the cultivation of the drug, to prevent its consumption.

The next important item in the Budget is the salt-tax, which from 2,602,670*l.* in 1858-9 rose to 6,227,301*l.* in 1874-5. It is argued in support of this tax that it is the only way in which a large majority of the population contribute to the necessities of the state, and that it is only right they should assist the revenue. Objecting to the opium revenue, and sensible of the difficulties which beset the finances of India, I cannot advocate any present alteration which would reduce the amount raised. At the same time it is a great misfortune that we should be obliged to levy a duty which falls on the poorest and most indigent of the population. A government should always strive to avoid taxing the necessaries of life. In this country the working classes pay by their consumption of tea, beer, and spirits, but these articles (unless we except beer) are luxuries and not necessities. Salt is a necessary of life, and it is deeply to be deplored that we should be obliged to place a duty upon it. Moreover, this duty is enormous. A ton of Cheshire salt, which the people of England may buy for 10*s.*, pays £8 17*s.* 3*d.* duty on being admitted into Bengal, and with freight and other charges costs 10*l.* 10*s.* to the people of that country. This cannot but restrict consumption, and we are told that no salt is used in agriculture, that the cattle are stinted of it, and that the poor along the sea-coast use salt-earth scraped from swamps washed by the sea, while in inland districts the scrapings from saltpetre pans are what thousands of families are reduced to consume. Much disease is said to be engendered by the scarcity of pure salt, and the trade in salt fish is hampered by the duty. It is certainly most unfortunate that we should have to depend for so large a revenue on this necessary of life, but the requirements of our Exchequer seem to leave us no alternative. The only questions are whether a reduction might not maintain the same amount of revenue by leading to increased consumption, and whether improvements might not be made in the mode of collection. As regards the first question, the poverty of the population may make it doubtful whether much can be expected from reduction, though it is a strong argument for it on the ground of humanity. The unequal incidence of the tax as collected in different parts of India has been condemned by Mr. Grant Duff in his account of his journey in *Macmillan.*[7]

The Customs raise the question of the duty on Manchester goods, of which we hear so much from

[7] Much valuable information on the salt-tax will be found in a pamphlet lately published by a friend of mine very conversant with every Indian question, Sir George Balfour, M.P.

Lancashire M.P.'s. The simple fact seems to be that the revenue cannot be dispensed with. The correspondence between Lord Salisbury and Lord Northbrook on this question was published just before I left India, and created much interest. The Viceroy seems to have treated the Secretary of State uncourteously, in not keeping him informed of his proceedings, and in passing an Act on this subject at Simla. Still, it must be borne in mind that the Council of Calcutta, who feel their responsibility in regard to the finances of India, could not see their way to the abolition of the duty; and, looking at the difficulty of maintaining a financial equilibrium, one does not see how they could arrive at a different conclusion. This affair is an illustration of the differences which may arise between the London and Calcutta Governments under the present system. Under the Company the Court of Directors exercised great power in questions of taxation; and, being for the most part old Indians, they regarded them from an Indian point of view. Now the Calcutta Government is under the control of the Secretary of State, who is, of course, responsible to Parliament, and if an influential body of members band together for any purpose, they may bring pressure to bear which it is difficult for any Minister to resist. In the present case the pressure is that of the great county of Lancashire, of which two of the present Secretaries of State are natives, and with which Lord Salisbury himself is connected by property. We have seen the Lancashire members—unaccompanied, it is true, by a single member not connected with that county—go in a body to Downing Street, to demand the abolition of these duties. The depreciation of silver has made it impossible at present to comply with their request; but the circumstance may well make us reflect whether the relations of the Indian Government with Parliament are in the position which might be desired.

The question of the income-tax was debated in India in 1871, and the tax was ultimately abandoned. There can be no doubt that the tax is unpopular, and the question arose whether the dissatisfaction it created did not counterbalance the advantage to the revenue. On this ground it was decided to abandon it, and after this decision it will be impossible, at all events for many years to come, to revert to it. Still, it may be a subject for regret that the attempt was not persevered in. The Hindoo dislikes new forms of taxation, but, when he is accustomed to them, he bears with submission, if not with cheerfulness, burdens which would terrify the inhabitants of other countries. The land-tax and the salt duty, which are both very high, if not excessive, are illustrations. The income-tax falls on the rich, who are able to make themselves heard; but had it been persevered in, it might ultimately have been acquiesced in, and it would have enabled us to do something to mitigate the severity of the salt-tax, which falls on the poor, who have no one to plead their cause. It must be admitted that there is a great consensus of opinion among those of Indian experience against an income-tax, and this opinion found utter-

P 2

ance in the Legislative Council, where Mr. Inglis stated "that for every man who pays the tax to Government, twenty pay to get off, and that for every rupee that is paid into the Treasury, another is paid to the subordinate officials; that is, that the natives of India paid last year upwards of 2,000,000*l*. as income-tax to the Government, and upwards of 2,000,000*l*. more as bribes." The corruption of the native agents the Government are obliged to employ was no doubt a difficulty in regard to this impost, as it is in many other questions. Still, it may be that the dislike entertained by Europeans to the income-tax led to the difficulties of its collection being exaggerated, and had the question been fairly encountered, it might have been a great assistance to our Indian finances. Be this as it may, when the attempt to impose it has been once abandoned it cannot be easily resumed.

A very intelligent officer engaged in the public works told me that he was an advocate for placing a tax on Hindoo marriages, which would be a source of revenue to the State, and would check what is a great abuse in India. A native who saves money expends it either on a tomb for himself or on a marriage-feast for his child. These marriage-feasts are a great source of income to the Brahmins. He said a man in his employment who did not spend as much as the Brahmins thought proper on a marriage, had all sorts of charges trumped up against him, and, had they not known the reason of the animus against him, they must have dismissed him, as they could only judge of the truth by the credibility of the witnesses. My friend recommended placing a heavy tax on these marriage-feasts, which he said would be a source of revenue to the Government, and would check a custom which is a source of much oppression to the Hindoos. It struck me that though there was much force in his remarks, yet that it was very doubtful whether this was a matter in which the Administration ought to interfere. The English govern a vast subject population alien to them in religion, habits and customs. It is their duty to study their feelings, and not to interfere with their customs, unless we are compelled to do so by strong moral considerations. As a Christian nation we were bound to dissever ourselves from all support of idolatry, and hence we withdrew from the management of the temples. Suttee was an abomination, giving a legal sanction to murder and suicide, which any civilized Government was bound to suppress. But most of the Hindoo customs, though they may be foolish in themselves, and fraught with evil to those who practise them, are not of a character which calls for the interference of the State, and when such is the case, it is right freely to allow them to take their course. We trust that the spread of the Gospel of Peace on earth and good-will towards men will ultimately overturn Brahminism, and we hope that extension of enlightenment and education will do much to improve the condition of the population ; but we do well to leave change to the operation of moral causes. Marriage-feasts are among the customs to which these remarks apply, and the Government is right to hesitate before it meddles with an institution which is not only supported by the most influential inhabitants, but is entwined with the traditions of the whole people.

An examination of the different items of income seems to leave little hope of any increase to the revenue. The question then arises, what can be done to reduce expenditure? The great item on this side the account is the army, which is stated to cost 16,000,000*l*. I have alluded to this subject in the last chapter, and it will be seen that whatever reductions may be made in the native regiments, the necessity of increasing the number of British officers, and of liberally pensioning disbanded sepoys, leaves little hope of much immediate saving. Railways in India have not been as remunerative as might have been expected, but we may hope that as their advantages become more appreciated by the natives, the income derived from this source will increase. We must bear in mind that it is by slow degrees that the Oriental changes his habits, and that it must be the work of time to teach him to make use of the new mode of transit. Another consideration is the great advantage they afford in a strategic point of view. We can now mass our troops on the hills in healthy localities, and be able to bring them to bear at short notice on any point which may be threatened. During the mutiny railways were scarcely known, and regiments had to be transported on the rivers or by dak. Ten thousand men now ought to be equivalent to more than twenty thousand in 1857. This in itself must be a source of great economy to the Exchequer, and justifies an outlay in their construction. Another consideration is very important. India is liable to famines, and occasionally dearth exists in one province while plenty is found in the next. It is of vital consequence, in such circumstances, to have the means of rapidly transporting food to the localities which are threatened. Here, as in other countries, the cost of the earlier railways was large, but this seems inseparable from the difficulties of commencing great undertakings.

The irrigation works in India have been recently attacked by Mr. Dacosta, in a very able pamphlet on Indian Finance, alluded to by Lord George Hamilton in his last Budget speech.[8] As regards these works, it is to be borne in mind that we are not to be solely guided by financial considerations, and that, when the very existence of the population of a district depends on irrigation, it may sometimes be necessary to construct works which cannot pay. Moreover, though a work may not be in itself remunerative, it may be so by increasing the land revenue. The Ganges Canal is an instance which, though only paying $2\frac{1}{2}$ per cent. *per se*, enhances the land revenue so as probably to produce 6.

The Home charges of the Indian Government de-

[8] I may mention that, though, in common with several much more distinguished men, I recommended Mr. Dacosta's pamphlet to the attention of M.P.'s, as "containing facts which demand the gravest consideration," with some of his conclusions I do not concur.

serve to be closely scrutinized. Mr. Fawcett has always urged, and urged with great reason, that many charges are debited to India which ought to be borne by the British Exchequer. The Committee of the House of Commons which sat from 1870 to 1873, owing to the dissolution of Parliament made no report to the House. What the report of that Committee might have been, had they been permitted to make one, may in many points be very doubtful. From what I know of the sentiments of my colleagues, I believe that, in the question of the Home Charges, they would by a large majority, perhaps unanimously, with the exception of the official members—those who were, who had been, or who expected to be connected with the India Office—have recommended that many of these charges should be transferred to the English Exchequer. The Home Charges are stated to be—

Interest on debt and guaranteed railways . .	£6,850,000
Pensions, annuities, allowances, and pay . . .	3,000,000
Payments to H.M. Treasury on account of the Post Office and Marine Departments; for Army and Political Missions	820,000
Troopships and passage of troops	350,000
Cooper's Hill College	25,000
Pension to Duleep Singh	19,335
Annuity to shareholders of the late Red Sea and India Telegraph Company	18,000
Administration, and minor departments . . .	250,000
Stores for India	3,000,000
All other payments	2,667,665
	£17,000,000

These items ought to be closely examined, with a view of ascertaining what portion legitimately belongs to India. There is a great temptation for any Government to transfer matters, which might give rise to unpleasant discussion in Committee of Supply, to the Indian Exchequer. The ball given to the Sultan is an illustration in point, and the charges of the Prince's visit ought to have been entirely defrayed by England. It is true the Indian Council is supposed to exercise the supervision over finance, which formerly belonged to the Court of Directors, but the position of the two bodies is entirely different. The Court of Directors owed no allegiance to the minister of the day, being elected by a constituency which, whatever its faults, was at least independent. They were therefore able to give an effectual protection to the interests of India, and, in one remarkable case (the recall of Lord Ellenborough), set at defiance the most powerful Government which has existed in England during the present reign. The Council, year by year, becomes more powerless to resist the Secretary of State, who, in his turn, very probably finds himself controlled by his colleague, the Chancellor of the Exchequer. Every Government has a strong interest to withdraw every possible expenditure from the cognizance of the House of Commons, and to transfer it to a body which has no real power. Were the accounts fairly adjusted between the Imperial and the English Governments, I cannot but think that a very large sum would be transferred from the latter to the former, and a proportional relief be experienced to the finances of the East.

The depreciation of silver was becoming serious at the time of my visit, and has since been alarming. The investigations of Mr. Goschen's Committee seem to prove that panic was one great element in the fall, and it is to be hoped that with returning prosperity the danger may pass away. Should this not be the case, the problem of East Indian finance will become increasingly difficult. Without this disturbing cause the revenue of India shows but little of that elasticity to which we are accustomed in England. As regards the three principal items, one could wish that changes or reductions could be made. Still, should peace continue, and should no unforeseen calamity disturb the calculation, the Indian Government are warranted in thinking the state of their finances, if not altogether satisfactory, at least gives no cause for grave alarm.

The condition of the lower classes in India is a matter of great interest. These teeming millions have to look for protection to a paternal Government, and, so far as Government can protect them, British rule has done so. Our reign has been a period of peace, and they have been allowed quietly to pursue their humble avocations. Still their lives are spent in the greatest poverty. In the hot climate of India, food is the only necessary of life, but the food they obtain is of the most meagre description. On this subject Sir R. Temple says, "The wages of labour may be generally stated at one to two annas[9] a day in Behar, two annas in Orissa, three annas in Northern Bengal, four annas in Central Bengal, five annas in Eastern Bengal, and six annas in Calcutta. During the last generation the rates ranged from one anna at the lowest to three annas at the highest, the lowest being the generally prevalent rate. On the whole, wages of labour have risen almost coincidently with the prices of common food. So far, then, we may hope that the lot of the labourer, always very hard, has not become harder of late. But we must sorrowfully admit that it is almost as hard as can be borne. A plain calculation would show that the wages will suffice for little more than the purchase of food, and leave but a slender margin for his simplest wants. In Behar, indeed, a comparison of prices with wages might indicate that his lot must be hard beyond endurance. It must be remembered, however, that wages are often paid in kind, especially for labour in the fields: the labourer and his family all work; the man, the woman, and the child receive each a dole of grain enough to sustain life; they could hardly get less now, and probably they never got more. Still, low as the condition of the labourer everywhere is, it is lowest in Behar. The industry and endurance, not only of the men, but of the women and children, in these classes are remarkable. One cause of the lowness of the wages is the comparative inefficiency

[9] Sixteen annas make a rupee; so, taking the rupee at two shillings, the anna is 1½*d*.

of the labour, which again is caused by the low and weak physique of these poor people, by reason of the poverty of their nurture, one cause acting and reacting upon another; while at the same time, despite the high rate of mortality, the high rate of births more than maintains the total number, which is probably increasing rather than decreasing. Another reason is, the large numbers of these people as compared with the employment available. There are three ways in which the condition of these classes can be ameliorated —(1) the increase of employment of various sorts as compared with the labourers; (2) the facility obtainable by the labourers for transferring their labour from one sphere or from one place to another; (3) the decrease of the number of the labourers relatively to the employment. In the first two ways we may certainly hope for improvement, which is, indeed, happily perceptible already. In the third way, improvement can only come from emigration, which, notwithstanding all our encouragement, is not as yet successful in these provinces. There is a class below even the labourers, namely, those who from infirmity are unable to work, and who have no subsistence save from that charity which is dispensed by all classes of the natives, according to their several means, with an unfailing generosity which may be counted among their national virtues."

Such is a feeling description, emanating from the highest authority, of the condition of the poor in Bengal. A stranger in India is struck by the way in which labour is employed where mechanical contrivances are substituted in Europe. The streets, for instance, are watered by coolies, who carry skins for the purpose, and I was informed that this is done because water-carts would be more expensive. The people are so poor and labour is so cheap that human beings become degraded almost to the condition of cattle. No wonder that there is a danger of residents in India, particularly of those who do not feel the responsibility of government, treating them as such. While I write, we hear of the case of the manslaughter of a native servant by an Englishman at Agra, and of the energetic Minute the new Viceroy has published on the subject. I think Lord Lytton deserves the gratitude of every friend of humanity for having maintained the principle, not too popular among the unofficial classes in India, that the natives are to be treated with the same consideration as Europeans, and deserve the same protection from the law. Those who settle in India with a view of seeking their fortunes are apt to take advantage of the poverty of the natives. Our position in Bengal is remarkable. In the North we have to govern men of warlike character; but the sixty millions of Bengalees—and the same remark applies to other parts of India—have always been ruled by other races, and passively submit to whatever befalls them. Hence the only security for their good government rests in the justice and moderation of the conquering power. Sir Richard Temple seems to pursue the wise policy of freely employing the natives in the public service. Looking at the way in which some of the independent

States have been governed by native statesmen, especially by Sir Salar Jung and Sir Madova Rao, it is to be wished that more use was made of native talent in the dominions of the Queen. Rules have been sanctioned by her Majesty's Government for the admission of natives of tried merit to appointments hitherto reserved for the Covenanted Service, and have been published; but the Lieutenant-Governor was directed by the Government of India to await further instructions before acting on them. He adds, "On receipt of such instructions I am ready to propose such action as may be necessary, and I trust that some native civil officers will be found who are worthy of the high confidence which such selection implies."

Under the head of "Instruction," Sir Richard Temple in his report gives an interesting account of the position of education in Bengal. Out of an expenditure of 390,000*l.* on education, 220,000*l.* are paid by the Government of Bengal, and 170,000*l.* by the people. The schools are divided into primary, secondary, and superior—generally private—schools, receiving a subsidy from the State on the condition of conforming to certain rules and submitting to Government inspection. A system of scholarships connects one class of schools with the other; and that system reflects great honour on the Government which has developed it, affording to every class the opportunity of rising in the world. "It has advisedly been made possible for a peasant boy, gifted with genius, learning in the most elementary village school, to win first a primary scholarship tenable in a primary school; then to win while there a scholarship tenable in a secondary school; then to win while there a scholarship tenable in a superior school, teaching up to the standard for entrance examination, and so to pass on to university membership; then, as an undergraduate, to win a junior scholarship, enabling him to study for and pass the First Arts examination, and to win a senior scholarship, further enabling him to study for and take a degree. All this he, originally destitute of means, may be able to do by State assistance; and if any persons are to be bound by ties of gratitude to a paternal government, he would be one of them. Having taken a degree, he would have a fair prospect of obtaining either a position at the Bar, or a place in the Native Civil Service of Government, either judicial or executive."[1]

In the primary schools education is entirely in the vernacular, and includes reading, writing, arithmetic, and simple mensuration. In the secondary schools the instruction is partly in the vernacular and partly in English, and includes the elements of natural philosophy, physical science, botany, and chemistry. The latest return shows the number of scholars to be 517,239, of whom 453,578 attended schools where English is not taught. This number may not seem large out of a population of 63,000,000 subject to the Bengal Government, but when we take into account the extreme poverty of the population it assumes a different aspect.

[1] Sir R. Temple's Report, p. 79.

The superior instruction, though partly in the vernacular, is mainly in English. The upper classes of Bengalees are most desirous to acquire the English language, though among the lower it is not nearly so commonly known as in Madras. Hence the University of Calcutta does not confer degrees in the vernacular or the classical languages of India. Looking at the position which English holds as the language of the governing class, a knowledge of it must be of the utmost consequence to any native who wishes to rise. Hence we find meetings of natives debating complex questions in English which would do no discredit to the most polished assemblies at home. The most superior and intelligent natives, of whom Kristodas Pal may be taken to be intellectually the leader, are most desirous to extend the knowledge of English. His own paper, the *Hindoo Patriot*, might compare advantageously in its style with many of its contemporaries in the United Kingdom.

Of course the position of women must be a bar to the advance of education. The seclusion to which they are condemned by the immemorial custom of the East makes it impossible for the Government to instruct them; and, when the mother of a family is ignorant, it cannot be expected that her children will be intellectual. The zenana missions are trying to improve the condition and education of females, but this must be a work of time. It will be seen by the statements which I have quoted that the British Government is earnestly striving to promote education in India.

CHAPTER VII.

BENARES, LUCKNOW, DELHI, LAHORE, AND AGRA.

The distance from Howrah to Benares is 475 miles; the fare, 44 rupees 8 annas. Having established myself in a comfortable carriage, I slept soundly, and next morning found myself traversing a country more picturesque than I expected, as the plains were not bare, and some graceful hills were visible. The line runs at a distance from the river, and traverses the great opium-producing province of Behar. It passes Patna, the great opium depôt for Behar; Dinapore, where Henry Martyn long pursued his apostolic labours; and Buxar, where Sir Hector Munro won a great battle. Madras time is generally kept on the Indian railways, I conclude as the most convenient which could be selected, as it is thirty-three minutes behind Calcutta time, seven minutes behind Allahabad, and thirty minutes in advance of Bombay. Sir Richard and Lady Meade were in the train, on their way to Hyderabad, where Sir Richard is appointed Resident. He very kindly invited me to visit him, and I greatly regretted that, having come so far north, and being limited for time, I was unable to accept this invitation, which would have enabled me to see something of the administration of one of the most important of the native states. About six in the evening we reached Mogul Serai, whence a branch line of six miles conducts to the Ganges, opposite Benares. Here I took a "garry," as the small carriage of the country is called, and crossed the broad stream of the Ganges, which looked beautiful under the light of a crescent moon, by a bridge of boats, which recalled the Rhine. This bridge of boats has to be removed when the river rises to its highest. After passing the bridge, I had to drive some two or three miles to the English cantonment, where I stopped at the United Service Hotel, of which I found myself the sole occupant. At Benares, as in other Indian towns, the Europeans reside outside in cantonments, frequently some distance off. The Indian hotel system is the same as the American. You are charged so much a day—six rupees in Calcutta and Bombay, five in the provinces—for board and lodging, including chota hazi, breakfast, tiffin, and dinner, which you pay whether you take your meals or not.

January 30th was Sunday, but in the afternoon I took a walk down to the city, passing the Government College—a very fine building—and the garden of Madhu Dass, where Warren Hastings was besieged when he visited the city. The greatest master of English composition in his most elaborate composition has described Benares:—"His (Warren Hastings') first design was on Benares, a city which in wealth, population, dignity, and sanctity was among the foremost of Asia. It was commonly believed that half a million of human beings was crowded into that labyrinth of lofty alleys, rich with shrines, and minarets, and balconies, and carved oriels, to which the sacred apes clung by hundreds. The traveller could scarcely make his way through the press of holy mendicants and not less holy bulls. The broad and stately flights of steps which descended from these swarming haunts to the bathing-places along the Ganges were worn every day by the footsteps of an innumerable multitude of worshippers. The schools and temples drew crowds of pious Hindoos from every province where the Brahminical faith was known. Hundreds of devotees came hither every month to die; for it was believed that a peculiarly happy fate awaited the man who should pass from the sacred city into the sacred river. Nor was superstition the only motive which allured strangers to that great metropolis. Commerce had as many pilgrims as religion. All along the shores of the venerable stream lay great fleets of vessels, laden with rich merchandise. From the looms of Benares went forth the most delicate silks that adorned the balls of St. James's and of Versailles; and in the bazaars the muslins of Bengal and the sabres of Oude were mingled with the jewels of Golconda and the shawls of Cashmere." Despite the changes of a century, much of this description continues to be true, and the flights of steps are still worn by the feet of innumerable worshippers. Benares, too, has the interest of being among the oldest cities in the world—perhaps, with the exception of Damascus, *the* oldest—which continues to be important. It is associated with the history of Buddha, though the religion of the place is no longer the worship of Buddha, but the worship of Brahma. The town consists of a labyrinth of lanes and alleys, possessing innumerable small shrines, through which it is very difficult to find your way. I succeeded in reaching one of the ghauts, or steep flights of steps, down which the people descend to bathe. It had been difficult to get there, but it was still more difficult to get back. However, at last I found myself outside these crowded houses, though I was late for evening service. Benares is more like a Turkish town than any I have visited, as Indian streets are generally wide. I dined with the Commissioner and Mrs. Carmichael, who escaped in great peril from their station to the hills in the time of the mutiny. Late in the evening the Maharajah of Benares, attended by two of his suite, called to take leave of Mr. Carmichael, who was starting next day on one of those circuits or tours of inspection which high Indian officials annually make. In the North a commissioner is appointed, having several collectors subordinate to him. The Maharajah was very courteous, invited me to visit him, and took me back to my hotel. Though he speaks no English, he is a member of the Viceroy's Legislative Council. He is a descendant of the celebrated Cheyte Sing.

Next morning Mr. Carmichael, though the preparations for his journey must have made it particularly inconvenient to him, had the great kindness to take me to the city. It is curious to see elephants and camels both employed in carrying loads. The number of small shrines is endless, as they are encountered at every turn, but neither the Hindoo temples nor the Mohammedan mosques are very large. The Golden Temple, though small, is handsome, despite the dirt, and the crowd of pilgrims and the "holy bulls" present a curious scene. We visited the palace of the Maharajah of Viziernagram, one of the most prominent of the natives of India at the present time. He is the ruler of a small principality in Madras, a member of the Viceroy's Council, and a Resident in the holy city of Benares. In each capacity he was incessant in paying his homage to the Prince of Wales. Personally I was much indebted to his Highness, as he lent us a carriage (the Commissioner's equipages having started on circuit) and a steam-launch to sail up and down the Ganges. This is the most wonderful sight of Benares, and certainly presents a magnificent spectacle. The splendid river sweeps past the city, which stands on elevated ground on the left bank. This plateau is covered with temples, with a few mosques and minarets interspersed. The ghauts descend from it, and the deluded Hindoos come pouring down in thousands, vainly thinking to wash away their sins in the sacred stream. In one place fires are lighted, consuming the bodies of the dead, whose ashes are thrown into the Ganges. Three or four of these pyres were blazing as we passed. The magnificent river and the picturesque buildings form a beautiful scene, which is made more striking by the crowd of worshippers; but it is sad to contemplate the folly to which idolatry reduces its victims. May a merciful God speedily bless the proclamation of His Gospel to those poor deluded creatures!

We sailed down nearly to the bridge of boats, and on our return noticed the window from which Cheyte Sing escaped. After enjoying this wonderful sail, we landed opposite the fine fort of Ramnuggar, belonging to the Maharajah of Benares, and visited the temple where the sacred monkeys reside, which is one of the most curious sights of the holy city. The Hindoos think it wrong to kill them, and consequently they accumulate till they constitute a nuisance to the neighbourhood. The same phenomenon is seen at the rock at Trichinopoly. Near this are stones marking the spots where Hindoo widows have committed Suttee. Benares is the metropolis of Brahminism, the great seat of Hindoo learning. There may be more splendid structures in the South, but the Hindoo everywhere looks with peculiar veneration to the holy city. The tide of Mohammedan conquest swept over it, but it still continued the peculiar seat of the ancient faith. After taking leave of my kind friend, I called on my way to the station on Mr. Sherring, whom I was not fortunate enough to find at home. This I much regretted, as I had been at college with him, and should like to have seen him, after so many years. He is now an eminent missionary, and the great authority on all that concerns the history and antiquities of Benares.

There is no railway bridge across the Ganges at Benares. The East Indian railway, by which I arrived, only goes to the southern bank, opposite the city. The Oude and Rohilcund, by which I left, leaves the town and keeps the north bank. The great road constructed by the Company from Calcutta to Peshawur passes through Benares. The Oude and Rohilcund is a thoroughly plebeian line—made for the people. It extends from Benares to Allyghur, a distance of 449 miles, with a branch to Cawnpore. It has only two classes, called the upper and lower. The upper charges about 1¼*d.* a mile, and the lower ¼*d.* The latter was pretty full, but for some distance I was sole occupant of the former. I was, however, joined by a Scotchman, who appeared to be the superintendent of the engine-drivers, who was eloquent on the impropriety of teaching natives to drive engines. His view seemed to be that India is to be farmed for the benefit of the English, and that it is the privilege of a Briton to come out and wring as much as he can out of the natives. For this purpose the Hindoo is to be kept down in every possible way, so that he may neither compete with his master in profitable occupations, nor attempt to disturb his rule of the country. My friend was a fair specimen of a large class who come to India—men often distinguished by correct and virtuous conduct in their intercourse with their own countrymen, but who regard the Hindoo as an inferior animal, to be trodden down for their own advantage. The antipathy justly excited against such people in the minds of the natives is one of the difficulties with which the enlightened statesmen who govern India have to contend. The travelling on the Oude and Rohilcund is not rapid, being only at the rate of fifteen miles an hour; so, having started at two, it was not till 11 p.m. that we reached Fyzabad, 120 miles, where I got a late dinner. Fyzabad was the old capital of Oude, and was the residence of Sujah Dowlah, the Nabob Vizier, with whom Hastings contracted his infamous treaty in regard to the Rohillas. After his son, Asaph-ul-Dowlah, built Lucknow, it continued to be the residence of the Begums or Princesses of Oude, whose misfortunes were immortalized by the eloquence of Sheridan.

At 5 a.m. on the morning of February 1, I found myself approaching Lucknow, where I took up my quarters at the Imperial Hotel, near the Kaiserbagh. The weather was very warm, which was a change, as at Calcutta the climate had been delightful, and punkahs were quite dispensed with. Captain Fendall Currie, a son of Sir Frederick Currie, the last Chairman of the East India Company, most kindly showed me the town. Lucknow is beautifully situated on the shores of the Goomti, and the fine trees which surround it formed a pleasing contrast to the parched plains over which the railway is carried. The family which long ruled over Oude, and which ultimately was permitted by the Company to assume the royal title, was Mussulman. Hence the city which they erected naturally attracted Mussulmen.

It grew rapidly, and is now the fourth city in India, with a population of 350,000. These people are mostly Mohammedans, though the inhabitants of the country districts are Hindoos. The House of Oude were among the worst of the rulers of India. The greatest blots on the escutcheon of Warren Hastings are his transactions in league with them. In subsequent days their misgovernment and their vices were a source of constant anxiety to the Company, and the ablest Indian diplomatists found themselves unable to secure justice to their subjects. At length Lord Dalhousie, no doubt without reluctance, as the transaction was in accordance with his general policy, decided that misrule had reached such a pitch in the unhappy kingdom, that it was necessary for the happiness of the population to depose a monarch who neglected his duties and devoted his time to the most cruel amusements, and to transfer his subjects to the dominion of the Company. It was a curious coincidence that at the very same moment popular feeling in England was denouncing the Emperor Nicholas in the most energetic language, because he asserted that the crimes and the misgovernment of the Turks gave foreign nations a right to interfere. As it was thought convenient to pursue one policy as regards Russia, and another as regards Oude, we did not trouble ourselves about consistency.

Lord Dalhousie carried out his policy, and probably the result may have been to promote the peace and prosperity of the ryots of Oude, but it was the precursor of that fearful outbreak which shook the British

Empire to its foundations. The Mohammedans had always chafed under the rule of the English, and when one of their greatest houses was dethroned, no matter how great crimes it had committed, they resolved to resist. When we are told by the advocates of Turkey that we are bound to defend that decaying Empire to conciliate the Mohammedans of India, we may remind them that the great outbreak of 1857 followed closely on the Crimean war. The fact is, that it is only a proportion of the Mussulmen of India who acknowledge the Sultan as Caliph. The propriety of the annexation of Oude was much debated at the time, one party insisting on the immorality of undisguised conquest, the other asserting that the misgovernment of the king was so atrocious, that it left us no alternative. I well recollect, shortly after the mutiny, in the spring of 1858, dining with a great Indian statesman, now long gone to his rest, and saying to him, "I suppose you think you had no alternative except to annex Oude?" His reply struck and surprised me: "We thought so at the time, but I think if we had to do it again we should find many reasons why it was not necessary."

The Kaiserbagh, or old palace of the kings, is now used by the talookdars, or landed gentry, on their visits to Lucknow. It is an enormous collection of rather tawdry buildings, in a dilapidated condition. The great object of interest is, of course, the Residency where Sir Henry Lawrence defended himself till he died of his wounds, where Inglis continued the defence, where Havelock and Outram, coming up, were in their turn besieged, and where Colin Campbell, Lord Clyde, ultimately released the harassed garrison. The hill on which it stood is turned into a garden, and every effort is made to protect and preserve the different places of interest, though the ruins suffer from the tropical rains. Inscriptions state what happened in each spot. Here is the banqueting-hall, which was turned into a hospital. Here is the doctor's house, where Lawrence breathed his last. Here is his grave, marked by the inscription, "Here lies Henry Lawrence, who tried to do his duty." Here is a monument to the brave men who fell. Wandering through the grounds, one everywhere encounters inscriptions to soldiers and civilians, their wives and children, who perished in that terrible siege—a siege which must always count among the most glorious episodes in English history—an episode never to be forgotten while the services of the British army in the Peninsula, at Waterloo, and in the Crimea are remembered by a grateful country. I much regretted not getting to the Alumbagh, a few miles off, where, on the retreat of Sir Colin Campbell's army after the relief of the Residency, Havelock died and was buried. I should like to have seen the grave of a hero, of whom, in the eloquent words of the *Times*, "we think as we think of Wolff on the heights of Abraham, of Abercromby on the Egyptian sands, and of Moore on the cliffs of Corunna." He was not only a hero, but a Christian; and his memory must ever be dear to his country.

I dined with Captain and Mrs. Currie, who previously drove me to the Wingfield Park, laid out by Sir Charles Wingfield, when Chief Commissioner of Oude; to the Martiniere, a great school founded by General Martini, who, having made a large fortune in the service of the Nabobs some fifty years ago, bequeathed it for the purpose of establishing educational institutions in Lucknow, Calcutta, and his native city of Toulouse; and to the Club, which the large English community—ladies as well as gentlemen—frequent, which is situated on the beautiful banks of the Goomti. The province of Oude is governed by a Commissioner, who is independent of the Lieutenant-Governor of the North-West Provinces. Like Burmah, Scinde, and some other provinces, it constitutes an independent government. The talookdars, or landowners, pay a heavy rent to the Government, which is assessed for a period of thirty years, when it is readjusted. Sir George Cooper, the Commissioner, was at this time absent on one of those tours of inspection which Indian Commissioners take through their provinces, moving about in tents, with all their suite.

On the afternoon of the 2nd, Captain Currie took me on an elephant to the native town. Riding an elephant is amusing, though for a long distance it must be fatiguing. They seem to be expensive luxuries, as I was told they cost six rupees a day to keep. Placed in a houdah on his back, we enjoyed a magnificent view of the mosques, tombs, minarets, and domes, rising in all directions amid luxuriant vegetation. The native town is dirty, like other Eastern cities, but the scenes in its streets are striking and picturesque. This vast city has grown up within the last century, and though the buildings are not substantial, they look very magnificent. We visited a mosque, or, as they call it here, a musjid, where great preparations were being made for an illumination the following evening, in commemoration of the Mohurrun, the great Persian festival which recalls the murder of Hussein, the grandson of the Prophet. I regretted that I could not remain to witness what thousands of coloured lamps must have constituted a most brilliant sight. In the fort is a room, said to be the largest in the world—larger than that at Padua. Unfortunately it is closed early in the afternoon, so I had to be content with contemplating it from outside. The utility of the fort in a military point of view is said to be a disputed point among authorities on such questions.

After taking leave of my kind friend, I left Lucknow in the evening for Delhi, taking the Oude and Rohilcund railway to Allyghur. In the train I met an opium agent, who told me that Oude produces 11,000 maunds of opium, nearly a quarter of the Bengal production. This goes to Gazeepore, where the Government opium-buildings for the province of Benares are situated. I find it admitted that it is impossible to prevent opium being sold illicitly, and hence it is producing demoralization among our own subjects. We passed Bareilly in the night, and breakfasted at Chandausi. The railway runs through Rohilcund, whose annexation to Oude is the most infamous transaction in the history of Warren Hastings. It crosses the Ganges Canal and the irrigation channels in connexion with it. From the slow pace at which we travelled, I was afraid of missing the East Indian train, but we arrived just in time. At the old fortress of Allyghur the Oude and Rohilcund meets the East Indian Railway. Here I took a return ticket to Lahore, with liberty to stop at any place I liked. The Indian lines are liberal in their arrangements about return tickets. The East Indian is a great contrast to the Oude and Rohilcund, as it travels at a good speed, and with greater luxury. At Gazeeabad, where the direct line proceeds to Lahore and Mooltan, you change trains for Delhi, which is thirteen miles distant. The city looks striking as it is approached across the Jumna. At Delhi I took up my quarters at the dak bungalow. These dak bungalows are established by Government along the main roads. In many places they are a convenience, as they provide lodging and food at fixed prices. In Delhi, I think, I should have done better to go to a regular hotel, especially as the weather was cold. This was a great advantage, as I was able to go about all day, and no longer compelled to waste several hours indoors. Though the North-West Provinces enjoy a bracing climate in winter, I understood that they suffer from heat in summer to a much greater extent than Calcutta or Madras.

The city of Delhi is remarkable in Indian history, but chiefly remarkable for the heroism which recovered it to England in 1857. It was the Mohammedan capital of India. The tide of Mussulman conquest swept over the North, but the power of the Crescent spent itself as it approached Cape Comorin. Hence its interests are all Mohammedan, while in the great cities of the South the remains are Hindoo. It is true there is a large Hindoo population, but it is a population over which the Mussulman had ruled for centuries. It followed that when the mutiny broke out—which, though joined in by the Hindoo sepoys, had been mainly organized by the Mohammedans—the first object of the rebels—an object which they successfully accomplished—was the seizure of Delhi, and the proclamation of the effete monarch whom the Company had continued nominally to recognize. The recapture of the city re-established British supremacy in India.

On February 4 I called on Colonel Cracroft, the Commissioner, who sent an old chuprassi, who had fought for the English in the siege, to show me the city. The district of Delhi has, since the mutiny, been removed from the government of the North-West, and added to the Punjaub. Lord Napier had lately been entertaining the Prince of Wales, and great reviews had been held to enable him to inspect the sepoy army, on whom he made a most favourable impression by the kindness he showed them.

The fort, which contains the palace of the Moguls, is very extensive. It is entered by two gates, called the Delhi and Lahore gates. The road through the latter leads into a curious corridor, above which the officer in command was murdered in the mutiny; as the Company maintained a guard round the person of the great Mogul. The place is now turned into barracks. The chief points of interest are the Dewan Aam, or Hall of Public Audience, which is open on three sides, and supported by pillars; the Dewan Khass, or Hall of Private Audience, a pavilion of white marble, where the Peacock Throne, of solid gold, formerly stood; the Pearl Mosque, a sort of Court chapel, and the king's baths of marble. These halls are not very large, and are now falling into decay; but in the days when those who were familiar with the glories of the Grand Monarque at Versailles were struck with wonder at their magnificence, they must have been very gorgeous.

The Jumma Musjid, or great Mosque, is situated on an elevated plateau. Three gates are reached by a high flight of steps, and lead into a magnificent court, on the west side of which the musjid is placed. A fine marble reservoir stands in the centre of the court, while two minarets flank the mosque. These command a very extensive view, though a strong wind raised the dust, and prevented it being as good as usual. The long corridor of the musjid, of white marble, curiously inlaid, is very fine, but the great feature is the splendid quadrangle. The handwriting of Ali and Hussein is shown, as also a hair from the beard of Mohammed, but I had not sufficient reverence for the memory of the prophet to care to see it. The Chandni Chouk, or great native street, is the habitation of jewellers and shawl merchants. In the afternoon I drove to the ridge, whence the attack on the town was commenced, which commands a fine view. It is marked by a monument to the heroes who, despite the tremendous odds against them, maintained the honour of the British arms. I next visited the cemetery, where many of those brave men sleep, particularly General Nicholson, who fell leading his men to the final assault in the moment of victory.

Delhi possesses a fine museum and extensive public gardens. I took a walk by moonlight, and saw musicians perambulating the streets in honour of the Mohurrun. It was curious to find the cold make one's fingers dead after the heat of Lucknow. My native guide looked perished with cold.

Next morning I drove to the Kootub Minar, a pillar eleven miles from Delhi. The road lies through a district

> "Where kings, in dusky darkness hid,
> Have left a nameless pyramid."

The whole region is crowded with tombs and ruins of tombs. There are tombs of emperors, there are tombs of viziers, and there are tombs of which the origin cannot be discovered. The ride recalls the Appian Way, though the tombs are larger and finer. The famous monument of Cecilia Metella would here look small. This scene, however, despite the glories of those great men and wise rulers, Baber and Akbar, has not the associations with our earliest years which gives such a charm to the Roman road. This is no place

> "Where each old poetic mountain
> Inspiration breathes around,
> Every shade and hallow'd fountain
> Murmurs deep a solemn sound."

These stones, though some may cover the ashes of men who governed wisely and well, for the most part tell a tale of oriental treachery and oriental cruelty. The Kootub, which is surrounded by a pretty garden, is a pillar which rises 238 feet above the level of the ground, has five galleries around it, and is ascended by 377 steps. Its origin is obscure, and it is a matter of controversy whether it was erected by the Hindoos or the Mohammedans. The view from the summit is very extensive over arid plains, which are lost in the distance, with endless ruins spread at your feet, and Delhi in the distance. A cold wind was blowing, which seemed to shake the pillar, and prevented my enjoying the view. Opposite the Kootub is a large unfinished minar, or pillar, and around are several objects of interest. A great mosque with five arches, in the court of which stands a remarkable iron pillar, the beautiful gateway of Alaoodeen, and the tombs of Iman Zamin and Adam Khan are in the grounds. Near this is the diving well, a pool eighty feet deep, into which a boy jumped from a considerable height. On my return I visited the tomb of Seftir Jung, a large structure in imitation of the Taj at Agra, now in bad preservation, a curious hall under twenty-five domes, a cemetery, containing the tombs of several royal and distinguished personages, some of them very ornate and beautiful, and the tomb of the Emperor Humayoon. The last is an enormous building, with a marble dome raised upon two magnificent terraces, which give it a grand appearance. On our return we passed Perrana, an old ruined city, built on some rocks above the plain. The number of ruined cities around Delhi show the changes which have taken place in the district.

In the afternoon I left Delhi for Mussouri, as I was anxious to see a hill station. The principal of these are Darjeeling, Nynee Tal, Mussouri, and Simla. Of these I should apprehend that Darjeeling, the summer residence of the Governor of Bengal, is the best worth a visit, as it commands a view of Mount Everest, the highest mountain in the world. Mussouri, however, is the most accessible, and on that account I was recommended to visit it.

The Scinde, Punjaub, and Delhi Railway extends from Delhi and Gazeeabad to Lahore, and is continued to Mooltan. The line is the same as the East Indian to Gazeeabad, from whence I proceeded to Saharunpore. The train seemed full of ladies and gentlemen who had been stopping at Delhi during the time of the Prince's visit. We passed Meerut, the great military station of this part of India, memorable as the scene of the outbreak of the mutiny. I had thought of spending Sunday at Saharunpore, but, finding from a clergyman I met in the train that there was no service there, but that there was a church at Mussouri, I decided to push on; so, getting a hasty supper at the station, I took my place in the mail-cart, which started at 11 p.m. The mail-cart was not the most luxurious conveyance I ever travelled in, and as the night was cold it was necessary to submit to a little inconvenience, especially as we were only protected by curtains. However, it was a beautiful moonlight night, and the road was good. We saw the cart going the other way upset, but the people did not appear to be hurt. We crossed several streams and a range of hills before reaching the town of Deyra, where a young gentleman who had been my companion from Saharunpore stopped. After a cold and sleepless night, I reached Rajpore at 5 a.m., where the mail-cart stops, and where I got from the Victoria Hotel a pony to take me up the mountain to Mussouri, a lovely ride. I reached the Himalaya Hotel in time for church, after which I enjoyed a view of the snowy range from a hill behind the town. In the evening I walked to a convent, which commanded an extensive mountain view. The long lines of charcoal fires burnt in the valleys looked picturesque as I returned after dark. The villages which make up the Mussouri station extend over a range of hills. Mussouri stands in the middle at a height of 6500 feet; Landour, to the east, which is the highest, is 7300; and the convent, of which I did not learn the height, is to the west. All these hills are covered with detached villas and buildings. Mussouri does not, like some of the other hill stations, enjoy the advantage of the summer residence of a Governor, though it is, however, frequented. High-class schools have been established here to save Indians from sending their children home for education. On Monday morning I walked up to Landour, where is a station for invalided soldiers. Here I spent an hour enjoying the view. To the south are wooded hills sloping down to the vast Indian plains, which, though to a certain extent destitute of that verdure which gives such a charm to the Italian valleys, are nevertheless very beautiful. To the north is the snowy range of the Himalayas, spreading round about one-third of the horizon. These magnificent mountains, some of which reminded me of Monte Rosas, the Breithorn, and Les Jumeaux, though not as high as those near Darjeeling, rise to the height of 25,000 feet. The panorama, though not superior to many I have seen in Switzerland, is magnificent and grand. It seems a pity the Alpine Club do not direct their attention to these gigantic summits. After enjoying this wonderful prospect, I strolled down through the woods to Rajpore, where, as well as at Landour, the Mohammedans were celebrating the Mohurrun by processions and music. At Rajpore I hired a conveyance to take me through the night to Roorkee. It was a kind of palanquin placed on wheels, and as it shut up, and I could lay down, I passed a comfortable night. The distance is forty-nine miles, most of the way along the same road constructed by the Company, which I had traversed before. The drivers push their horses along, though changing is a slow process.

I arrived about 7 a.m. on the morning of the 8th at Roorkee, where I was most kindly entertained at the Thomason College by Captain and Mrs. Cunningham. The Thomason College was named after Mr. Thomason, formerly Lieutenant-Governor of the North-West Provinces, and is an institution where students, whether Europeans, East Indians, or natives, are instructed in engineering. It is officered by Royal Engineers—Major Lang, the Principal, Captain Cunningham, the Vice-Principal, and their assistants, all belonging to that corps. It is one of those institutions which reflect much honour on the Indian Government, while the progress made by the students does much credit to the heads of the college. I was shown the Government workshops by Mr. Campbell, the Superintendent. They are very extensive, employing 1000 natives.

Sir William Muir had strongly advised me to see the Ganges Canal, and particularly the works between Hurdwar and Roorkee. With this object I started at night, in a dooly, a sort of palanquin, slung from a pole carried by two men before, and two behind. I had eight bearers at a rupee each, who took turns. I was interested in the expedition, as it was a specimen of the old mode of travelling in India. You recline at full length, and though in a long journey it would be uncomfortable not to be able to sit up, yet in travelling by night, when one wants to sleep, it is pleasant enough. At Myapoor, two miles from Hurdwar, where the dam and the regulator for the canal are placed, my dooly stopped; but I preferred remaining in it for the rest of the night, as I was very sleepy. Myapoor is the scene of a great decennial fair, where holy dervishes resort, and sit on pillars, which are shown.

I rose at dawn, and walked on to Hurdwar, a holy

city of the Hindoos; from its temples, shops, stalls, and strange costumes, more thoroughly Indian than any I had seen. It was curious to be among a crowded population, unable to speak a word in common with any one. Here the Ganges comes rushing out of a ravine in the mountains with great velocity, and crowds of deluded heathen here, as at Benares, come to the bathing-ghaut, thinking to wash away their sins in the sacred stream. The outsides of the temples are curiously carved and painted, and the people thronging the streets present a picturesque appearance. I enjoyed wandering through this interesting city, and then returned to Myapoor, where Lieutenant Clibborn, an officer engaged on the canal, hospitably entertained me. While we were at breakfast, news was brought that an elephant, riderless, and covered with blood, had come to a place near. It was feared that a tiger had attacked the party upon him and killed them. I afterwards understood that the account here given me was in the Allahabad paper; but it did not state whether the fate of the poor riders had been ascertained, and I never heard.

Lieutenant Clibborn took me in his boat to Pathu, about half way to Roorkee, whence I proceeded in the dooly. He told me, and it is an illustration of the extreme cheapness of labour in India, that natives placed in very responsible positions on the canal—in fact, on whose care and coolness the safety of this great work depends—only get six rupees a month. Labour would seem to be much cheaper here than in Bengal.

The Ganges Canal was one of the most wonderful works of John Company, and effectually disposes of the allegation that that much-abused individual was indifferent to his duties as a ruler. It was constructed by Colonel Sir Proby Cautley, and was opened in 1854. The regulator at Myapoor controls the quantity of water which enters the canal, which is a large body of water running three miles an hour. A few miles lower we turned into a side canal, constructed with locks for traffic, though it is not much used for this purpose. In several places the water rushes through weirs constructed for the purpose, while in others torrents, which in the wet season are large and powerful, are carried over the canal on aqueducts. Several fine bridges span the canal. At thirteen miles from Myapoor, and six from Roorkee, it makes a bend, and soon afterwards a river is allowed, when necessary, to cross it on a level, which is considered a wonderful triumph of engineering skill. In other places, and particularly on approaching Roorkee, the canal is carried on aqueducts over streams. Though the chief works are between Myapoor and Roorkee, it extends to Cawnpore, over 300 miles below. It has 654 miles of main channel, and 3040 of distributing lines. It cost 22,800,000 rupees, and brings in a net income of 543,000 rupees, or about 2½ per cent.,[1] though probably, taking into account the increase of the land

[1] I quote the figures as they were given me at Roorkee. I see Mr. Thornton, C.B., represents the canal as yielding 4·88 per cent.

revenue, it pays 6 per cent. Whether it pays or not financially, there can be no question that it promotes the prosperity of the people.

I reached the college in time for dinner, and, on the morning of the 10th, Major Lang, who had been on a tour with some of his pupils, returned. He is a distinguished officer, who was engaged in the siege of Delhi and in the relief and capture of Lucknow. His wife and children were away in England, and he was only one of many I met whom public duty retains in India at a distance from their families. We do not sufficiently appreciate the sacrifices made by those who serve their country in the East. In the afternoon I took leave of my hospitable friends, and proceeded by dak to Saharunpore, thirty miles off, where I arrived about 9 p.m., and proceeded through the night to Lahore. We passed Umballa, the station whence the Calcutta grandees take dak for Simla—the Viceroy's hill station, and Loodiana, the great missionary station, and crossed the Sutlej, the river which was our boundary before Sir John Hobhouse forced on the Affghan War. About eleven next day I arrived at Lahore, where I stopped at Clark's Hotel.

Lahore was the capital of Runjeet Sing, and, since the subjugation of the Punjaub, has been the chief city of that province. It was here that Sir John (now Lord) Lawrence ruled during the mutiny; here he maintained tranquillity among the warlike population, and hence he sent forth the battalions which retook Delhi. It is situated on the Ravee, one of the five rivers from which the country receives the name of the Punjaub, pun meaning five. In approaching, you pass Meean Meer, a great encampment for troops, and see many large tombs. Like other Indian cities, the European population reside in bungalows covering a large space. The cantonment possesses a large hall and a museum of curiosities. The native town has the houses built close together like the cities of the Levant, unlike any I have seen in India except Benares. On its further side are the mosque, the fort, and the gardens and tomb of Runjeet Sing. The mosque, though very much out of repair, is fine, with an enormous quadrangle. The minarets are heavy towers, very different to the graceful structures one admires in Constantinople and Damascus. The gardens and tomb of Runjeet Sing are situated between the mosque and the fort. In the midst of the gardens, which are pretty, is a sort of kiosk, which I was told was the Prince's reading-room. It is of beautiful marble. The tomb is close to the wall and is very splendid. The body reposes under a dais, over which is a marble dome, with paintings by native artists, and gilt outside. The priests who surrounded it seemed interested to hear that I often saw his son in London. The fort contains his palace, which has some rooms gorgeously painted. It is a very extensive range of buildings, now turned into a citadel, with barracks in which both British troops and Seiks are quartered. The view from the top is very pretty, extending over boundless plains. On every side are tombs and Oriental buildings, while the native city lies below on one side, and the river at a little distance on the other.

At dinner at the hotel I met Major Harrington, the Commissioner of Gujranwala, who recommended me to see the bridge over the Chenab at Wazirabad, recently opened by the Prince, and kindly wrote to his deputy there to make arrangements. I accordingly started early on the 12th by the Punjaub Northern Railway, a narrow-gauge line, which is to be superseded by a broad-gauge, now making. The railway follows for sixty-two miles the line of the Company's great road from Calcutta to Peshawur, and runs over vast barren plains. It was curious to watch the long strings of camels proceeding along the road. We passed a native regiment on march. Gujranwala is a town of 50,000 inhabitants, which looked fine. At Wazirabad I was met by Syed, the Mohammedan deputy collector, who very kindly accompanied me across the bridge. As I had only two hours to see the bridge I was anxious to have taken a trolly and gone, but Mr. Danvers, the Government Director of Indian Railways, was on a tour of inspection, and of course everything had to give way. He had a special train over the bridge, in which he allowed us to ride. The Punjaub rivers in the dry season have but little water; but when the floods come down from the mountains, they run with great velocity and frequently change their channels. Hence the necessity of very long and strong bridges. The one in question over the Chenab, which is built on piers stretching across the wide bed of the river, is a mile and three quarters long—with the exception of that of the Grand Trunk Railway of Canada over the St. Lawrence, the longest in the world. It commands a fine view of the snowy range of the Himalayas. Having crossed in the Director's carriage, which stopped for the party to examine everything, we procured a trolly to take us back. These trollies, which are driven by coolies at a great pace, are much used on this line. On the return we were in considerable danger. Some native workmen had left a piece of wood on the road, which threw our trolly off the line. As the bottom of the road is open, we ran a risk of falling between the timbers and being dashed against the piers of the bridge. By the great mercy of our Heavenly Father we alighted on our feet unhurt, and, getting into another trolly, returned safe to Wazirabad. Meantime the train had left for Lahore, and I had to pass the rest of the day at Wazirabad. My friend the magistrate was most kind, taking me about the town, which is a good specimen of India, showing me a school under the management of the Presbyterians, where the children read English, and some curious gardens. I dined and slept at the dak bungalow, where I met an officer *en route* for Peshawur, where we maintain a large body of troops.

On Sunday morning I returned to Lahore, and as I could not arrive in time for church, I stopped at Shahdara, the next station, and walked on, visiting *en route* the tomb of the Mogul, Sultan Jehangeier. An immense square, used for railway works, leads into a similar square, used partly as a garden, partly to grow corn, which contains the tomb in the midst. The building is flanked by four ponderous minarets. Painted corridors lead to the tomb, which is very elaborate, with marble and inlaid stones.

I crossed the Ravee by a footpath suspended under the railway bridge, which, though it is shorter, resembles that at Wazirabad, and had a dusty walk to the hotel. In the evening I attended service in a tomb fitted up as a chapel. At dinner my only companion was an Italian artist on his way to the Vale of Cashmere. Early on the 14th I started homewards, spending the day at Umritsur, to see the Golden Temple. Here I was very kindly entertained by General and Mrs. Taylor. General Taylor, the Commissioner here, is a very distinguished officer, who has seen much service in the Punjaub, and who has been very active in promoting missionary labours. At their house I met Colonel and Mrs. Bousfield, who I found were near connexions of friends of mine. The Colonel, who is chief of the police for the district, most kindly gave up the day to show me Umritsur. Driving through some lovely gardens, we entered the native city, which looked curious from the remnants of painted hangings placed before the shops in honour of the Prince's visit. The great sight of Umritsur is the Golden Temple, the most beautiful I saw in India. It stands in the midst of a large piece of water, which reminded me of the Hague, and is covered with gold beat on to plates of copper. In this temple is kept the copy of the sacred book of the Sikhs, which is encased in several coverings. Walking round the tank, and passing a Seik prostrated at full length, we entered the shrine where the worshippers were sitting round the sacred book, uttering a low monotonous chant. At Colonel Bousfield's request the sacred volume was uncovered. Covering after covering was removed, till at last the book appeared, when the worshippers devoutly prostrated themselves. Some of the contents was read to us. It is so far satisfactory that this worship is paid to a book and not to an idol, but it is lamentable to see devout men wandering in darkness and rejecting the only source of peace. Over the court where the priests sit are elaborately-painted galleries surmounted by the gilded dome. From a minaret near, one looks down on the beautiful temple which stands in the middle of the tank, joined to the bank by a causeway. The view in other directions is over the Indian plains, here looking greener than usual, which are lost in the distance, not a hill being seen anywhere. Opposite the causeway is another temple, where a yet more sacred book is kept, which is only opened once in the year. Here the rites are gone through for admitting men as Sikhs. The paintings are curious, one of them recording a strange tradition. A Sheik Goree, a priest king, went to Mecca, and fell asleep in the court of the Caaba, as the great mosque there is called, with his feet towards the shrine. The Mohammedan guardian, horrified at such profanation, tried to turn him round so that his head might be towards the Caaba. As often, however, as he was turned, the mosque turned too, so that he remained in the same relative position. The story commemorated by this picture shows how little respect the Sikhs have for Mohammed.

After a very pleasant day with my kind friends, I proceeded by the night train to Agra.

The Punjaub is a province of the greatest interest in the consideration of Indian questions. Its inhabitants are not an effeminate race like the Bengalees, but hardy and warlike mountaineers. Macaulay in a graphic passage describes what in various ages has been the course of invasions of India. He says, "The people of Central Asia have always been to the inhabitants of India what the warriors of the German forests were to the decaying monarchy of Rome. The dark, slender, and timid Hindoo shrank from a conflict with the strong muscle and resolute spirit of the fair race which dwelt beyond the passes. There is reason to believe that, at a period anterior to the dawn of regular history, the people who spoke the rich and flexible Sanscrit came from regions lying far beyond the Hyphasis and Hystaspes, and imposed their yoke on the children of the soil. It is certain that, during the last ten centuries, a succession of invaders descended from the west on Hindostan; nor was the course of conquest ever turned back towards the setting sun, till that memorable campaign in which the cross of St. George was planted on the walls of Ghizni." The dangers which we may have to encounter in India can only be looked for from the brave tribes which inhabit the mountain regions. In our troubles in the mutiny they were faithful to us, and probably, as long as they are on our side, we have nothing to fear from any other race in India. Should, however, they ever become disaffected, and particularly should these gallant soldiers ever be trained by hostile European officers, our Indian Empire may have to meet a severer struggle than it has ever yet encountered. Hence the immense importance of the warlike population of the Punjaub being well governed.

I spent the 15th travelling towards Agra, following as far as Allyghur the same route which I had previously traversed. In the carriage was a gentleman who was travelling without stopping from Mooltan to Bombay, preferring 1800 miles of railway to the steamer down the Indus. At a junction called Toondla, a branch line conducts to Agra. The view of the Taj rising from the plain, as we approached the city in the twilight, reminded me of St. Peter's towering over the Campagna. The railway is carried across the Jumna by a fine bridge. About seven o'clock I reached Laurie's Hotel. Next day I visited what is held by common consent to be the most wonderful monument in India, the masterpiece of Mogul magnificence, the Taj Mahal. It was erected by Shah Jehan, the son of Jehangeier, as the last resting-place of his wife, Momtaz Mahal, about the middle of the seventeenth century. A court, surrounded by numerous small cupolas, contains a splendid gate, which leads into a beautiful garden, cultivated with much care. From the gate the magnificent marble dome is seen raised on two terraces, and flanked by four graceful minarets. Passing up the centre walk, which has canals of water in the middle, you reach the first terrace, which has the garden on the south, the Jumna flowing below on the north, and large mosques on the east and west. The upper terrace has a minaret at each corner, and from it rises the tomb, with a gilded crescent on its summit, and with several minor domes surmounted by gilt ornaments glittering in the sun. Entering through elaborately-carved gates, you reach the centre, where a small tomb marks the grave of the queen, and a larger one that of her husband, the whole brilliant with carving and inlaid stones. Over this the dome rises to the height of 270 feet. The whole is of marble and presents an appearance of incomparable grandeur. The fort contains the Moti Musjid, a beautiful marble mosque, and the old palace, which is very magnificent with elaborate carvings and beautifully inlaid stones. The fort is situated on the Jumna between the city and the Taj, and its high walls enclose a great space.

In the evening I took a walk through the native city, which is a good specimen of an Indian town. The natives live huddled together, often sleeping out of doors, so that a large population can be crowded into a small area. A bridge of boats crosses the Jumna, but, owing to the shifting channel of the stream, it must be a constant difficulty to keep it in repair. I entered the court of the great mosque, which did not look remarkable, except for size, but the people about made signs to me to go no farther. I did not understand the reason, as I have generally found the musjids freely open. Agra and Delhi were the capitals of the Mussulman power, and from them the Moguls ruled India. Some of these sovereigns were great men and beneficent rulers, but on the whole the dynasty oppressed the large subject population of Hindoos. Such magnificent works as the Taj can only be constructed at enormous expense, and the taxes wrung from the poverty of the people were spent in useless extravagance—not in beneficent works of public advantage. I dined with Mr. Simson, the collector, and met some young civilians, who complained of the slow promotion in the service in the North-West Provinces.

On the 17th I started for Futtehpore Sikr, the residence of Akbar, the greatest and best of the Mogul Princes. I had a phaeton with one horse, which was changed three times for others previously sent on. For this I paid eighteen rupees. For twenty-two miles one traverses the usual unending plain without a hillock to be seen, though diversified by occasional trees and rendered picturesque by strings of camels, carts drawn by bullocks, Hindoos with painted faces and gorgeous costumes, and women with huge rings in their noses. At length the city comes in sight, the view of which reminded me of Assisi as seen from the plain below. It was once very extensive, it being seven miles round the walls. Now it is completely deserted, with the exception of the two villages of Futtehpore and Sikri. Government expends 1200*l.* a year in keeping the ruins in repair. The mosque is very large, with a court 428 feet long by 406 broad, and with a gateway 140 feet high, which towers over the surrounding country, commanding a view where, for a wonder, some hills are visible. It contains the tomb of Sheik Selim Christi, a holy man to whom Akbar was attached, one of whose descendants now acts as guide. The sheik rests in an elaborate tomb, surrounded by other members of his family. The mosque covers part of an elevated plateau, the remainder of which is occupied by the palace containing the halls of Akbar and the houses of his wives. This wonderful specimen of the magnificence of Akbar has a garden of five terraces, one over the other, supported on columns. The palace is entered by a gate, called the elephants' gate, from two figures carved over it, while near it is a tower called the elephants' tower, from figures of tusks upon it.

Returning to Agra, I started through the night for Jeypore, a distance of 149 miles by the Rajpootana State Railway, which, though it runs through the Rajpoot States, is an Indian Government line. I was anxious to see a native State, and Jeypore was the most accessible, though, as its sovereign is the most enlightened prince in India, I should have preferred one which would have been a more average specimen. Gwalior, the capital of Scindia, would have suited me better, but there is no railway to it. Rajpootana is a collection of petty principalities under their native princes, while an English resident is accredited to each Court. There is also a Chief Commissioner of the Viceroy for these States. The line passes several towns memorable in Indian history—Bhurtpore, the scene of Lord Combermere's glory, and Deig, where Lord Lake won a great victory. Reaching Jeypore in the morning, I breakfasted with Colonel Beynon, the Resident, who told me that the territory of Jeypore has a population of 2,000,000. He seems to have had much trouble about Dacoitee, the system of robbery which exists in India. I visited the public gardens, where it was interesting to see the Maharajah has erected a statue, as a token of gratitude to "his friend, Lord Mayo." This made me think that the services of the late lamented Viceroy have been very inadequately recognized by his country. A generous opponent has conferred an earldom on Lord Northbrook, who has returned to enjoy the homage of his admirers. Surely it would have been a graceful act in Mr. Gladstone to have bestowed an English Peerage on the son of one who, though differing from the late Prime Minister in politics, governed India to general satisfaction, and fell a victim to his devotion to the service of his Sovereign and country.

I saw the hospital, the palace, and the college. The palace contains two large durbar halls, which had been splendidly fitted up for the Prince's visit. A succession of terraces, one over the other, the highest of which has a fine view, are curious, as are the large gardens. The college does the Maharajah great credit. I was surprised and gratified at the facility with which the boys read the Waverley novels, and at the knowledge which they showed of English. The school of art did not seem to be equally successful, but both testify to the anxiety of his Highness for the improvement of his subjects. The streets of Jeypore are very picturesque, as the houses are curiously painted. They are clean and wide, and the town is surrounded by a wall like that of Delhi. I saw an elephant paraded in the gorgeous trappings in which the Prince of Wales had ridden upon him, and a collection of tigers at the end of one of the streets. I heard that they sometimes prowl down to the neighbourhood of the town. Jeypore is surrounded by fine hills, and presented a great contrast to the flat country through which I had lately been passing. On one of these, a fine old city called Ambere is situated, which I much regretted I could not visit, but my time was limited, and I therefore returned to Agra through the night.

On the 19th, after breakfasting with my kind friend Mr. Simson, I drove to Secundra, the tomb of the great Akbar, which is very large. On the top of several terraces a small screen surrounds a sarcophagus. The building is grand and Oriental, but it is in bad repair, and looks poor after the Taj. I felt much indebted to Mr. Pye, who advised me at Amoy to leave Agra till the last, as the Taj was far the finest sight in India. With great admiration for the vast temples of the South, for the picturesque character of Benares, for the magnificence of Lucknow, Delhi, and Lahore, and for the gorgeousness of Umritsur, I still think this advice was good, and commend it to any future traveller. Dr. Tytler, the Governor, showed me over the gaol, which contains about 2500 prisoners. They are employed in useful work, such as mat-making, and make their own clothes. I was told that burglary is the most common offence for which they are committed. There are also many confined for infanticide, which they do not consider a crime. Hindoos are to Mussulmen in the prison as seventy to thirty, about the same proportion as in the population. Some of the best-conducted prisoners are promoted to small appointments in the establishment. It was sad to contemplate this large body of human beings, condemned for their crimes to a wretched existence here, and with no hope hereafter. After again visiting the Taj, and taking a last look at its glories, I left Agra for Cawnpore, a journey of 157 miles. I reached my destination about 1 a.m., and stopped at the Railway Hotel.

Next morning, being Sunday, I was interested in attending service in the Memorial Church, erected in memory of those who fell during the mutiny, and recently consecrated. It stands within what was Wheeler's intrenchment, and is surrounded, within and without, with inscriptions to the memory of those who fell. The congregation was chiefly composed of military men—soldiers from the neighbouring barracks attending. After church, I walked to the Memorial Gardens, where the fearfully famous Well of Cawnpore is situated, into which the bodies of the victims of Nena Sahib were thrust. It is now surrounded by walls, and surmounted by an angel by Marochetti. The gardens are prettily laid out, and several monuments and inscriptions, some of them marking the graves of those who died, are interspersed through them. The scene is sadly memorable in the history of British endurance and British courage. Cawnpore is situated on the Ganges, and it is to it that the canal extends from Hurdwar, running through the main street. Cawnpore was the scene of Henry Martyn's last missionary labours in India, and here he preached to the heathen in their own tongue. One may contrast the state of India in his time with the present, and ask if Christianity has made the progress which might have been hoped. There are a good many native Christians, particularly in the South, but we may well pray for a greater blessing on the labours of God's servants. As regards the English community, the forms of religion seem as well observed as in England, we may hope, in many cases, sincerely—very different, at all events, to the neglect which once prevailed.

CHAPTER VIII.

BOMBAY, AND HOME.

I PROCEEDED through the night to Jubbulpore, the termination of the East India Railway, and the commencement of the Great Indian Peninsula. I was told that railways are doing much to break down caste in India, as all castes find themselves obliged to mingle in the carriages. If this is the case, they are effecting a very difficult task, as the feeling of the Hindoo about caste is one which has to be considered and respected in all transactions with them.

At Allahabad, the great junction station, we changed carriages for Jubbulpore. Allahabad is situated near the confluence of the Jumna with the Ganges, both which rivers come out of the great mountain chain in the Dehra Doon district, and pursue a parallel course for more than 400 miles. From its situation, it is a point of much strategical importance, and has become the capital of the North-West Provinces. Agra formerly held this honour, but, having been cut off from communication with Calcutta during the mutiny, the seat of the Lieutenant-Governor was transferred to

Allahabad, which had maintained intercourse by the river. The construction of railways has increased its importance, as lines converge here from the Punjaub, Calcutta, and Bombay.

The Jumna looked very fine as we crossed it by starlight, and in the morning I found the country covered with fine trees, with pretty hills in sight—a great contrast to what I had recently passed through. After a journey of 318 miles, I reached Jubbulpore about half-past eight on the morning of February 21st, and stopped at the Great Northern Hotel. The attraction of Jubbulpore is the Marble Rocks, situated about twelve miles from the town. Driving through a pretty country, we turned into a beautiful valley, and reached the bungalow built for the reception of travellers. The view from the terrace behind it is very charming, particularly in the arid climate of India. I first walked to a curious Hindoo temple, and then proceeded to the Falls of the Nerbudda. They are only forty-five feet high, but the body of water is considerable, and after its descent, the river rushes through a chasm in the rocks for a great distance. It then enters a small lake surrounded by hills and woods. Returning to the bungalow, I descended to the lake, where I took a boat up the river into the chasm, which is very striking from the huge marble rocks which enclose it. This channel has been worn by the stream in the course of ages. Near the Falls an inscription marks the grave of an unfortunate Englishman who, being attacked and stung by bees, fell into the river and was drowned.

Leaving this beautiful spot I returned to Jubbulpore, which is a great military station, where the tents of the native troops cover the plains around. At dinner at the hotel I met some officers, one of whom described to me the battle of Ferozeshah. The ammunition was spent, and affairs looked desperate. He was present when Lord Hardinge, thinking all was lost and that he must fall where he stood, took off his decorations and gave them to his son, who was a civilian, saying, "Carry these home to your mother." The Sikhs, however, were suspicious of some deep design from our firing ceasing, and when the cavalry charged as a last effort they retreated.

Next morning I proceeded to Bombay, a distance of 616 miles. The people of the Bombay Presidency are very proud of the Great Indian Peninsula Railway, which runs to Jubbulpore in the direction of Calcutta, and to Rachoor in that of Madras. It seems a comfortable line, and the way the stations are built and nice gardens laid out around them is very pretty. The carriages are built for a hot climate, so that I found them rather cold at night. People told me I could have no idea of India without being there in summer. The heat must be terrific, particularly in those parts which are far removed from the sea. It is not uncommon for natives as well as Europeans to die of heat apoplexy in railway journeys, and I was told that coffins are kept at the stations, to provide against what is a not unfrequent occurrence.

Our route lay through the Central Provinces. Some

of these are administered by commissioners, and there are several small native chiefs. To the north lay the territories of Holkar, the great Mahratta prince. The country was more pleasing than that through which I had recently travelled, and some pretty hills were in sight during much of the day. I was in company with a doctor in the Indian army, who told me that in 1857 he was stationed near Delhi, and the Collector remarked to him that he did not like the look of the natives, as they were either uncivil or too civil. Soon afterwards this gentleman was removed to another station, but his successor, refusing to leave his post and escape, was murdered with his wife and child. My informant himself escaped by hard riding on a camel. At daylight, on the 23rd, we were in a wild, hilly country, still in the table-land of Central India. The great chain of mountains, which is the watershed of the peninsula, is near the western coast. Hence the great rivers run east into the Bay of Bengal. We soon began to descend the Thull Ghaut, which conducts the railroad to the low lands along the sea. In the midst of the descent the train runs into a siding, the engine is turned round, and then takes the train the reverse way. The scenery of the ghaut is fine, though not particularly remarkable, and the ride on approaching Bombay is pretty. We reached the capital of Western India about half-past eleven, and I proceeded to the Byculla Hotel.

Byculla is situated at one end of Bombay, and I found the hotel, which is kept by Parsees, convenient, as being near the P. and O. wharf at Mazagon, and the Governor's house at Pareil. Watson's Hotel, on the esplanade, is, I believe, preferred by people who like luxury. In reaching Bombay I again found myself in a hot climate, and all the appliances for obviating heat are necessary. Punkahs are required at meals, and mosquito curtains at night. I drove down to the city, where I got money, and engaged my passage in the next steamer for Venice. I was not fortunate in meeting with those to whom I had letters, except the Governor, Sir Philip Wodehouse, who invited me to a ball in the evening. When I arrived at Government House he was most kind; and I much enjoyed an hour's conversation with a statesman who knows much of India, and whose colonial experience is perhaps unrivalled.

Next day I made an excursion to Poona, the old capital of the Peishwa, my object being to see the most wonderful engineering work in India—the Boer Ghaut. At Kallian junction, twenty-three miles from Bombay, the line to Poona and Madras leaves that to Allahabad and Calcutta, and at Kurjat begins to ascend for seventeen miles to Lanoli. The railway is a wonderful work, not unworthy to be compared with the Semmering or the Brenna. It passes through twenty-four tunnels, mostly cut out of the solid rock. As on the Thull Ghaut, the engine has in one place to be reversed. The scenery was grand, and must be very beautiful after the rains, but at this time everything was burnt up. At Lanoli, seventy-nine miles from Bombay, the top of the ghaut is reached, and the line proceeds through a dry and level country for forty miles, till it arrives at Poona, which looked like an oasis in the desert. Shortly before approaching the city, the palace of the Governor of Bombay, situated a few miles off, is visible. It was too late, on my arrival, to see much of Poona, which appeared to be a very fine town. At dinner, at the Napier Hotel, I sat next a lady and gentleman who had come in by the train. I found the gentleman was a very superior man, and in the course of conversation learned he had been to Mecca. Upon this I said, "Then you must be Captain Burton." He said he was Captain Burton, and told me that, not having been in India since his younger days in the Madras army, he was now visiting it. He had been seeing the Rock Temples, and was now on his way to Hyderabad and Madras. He talked about the Euphrates Valley railway scheme, which he says should run from Tripoli by Baalbec and Palmyra. I apprehend this scheme will have to wait till the Eastern question is more settled than it is at present.

Next day I returned to Bombay by the same route, but I was not sorry to have a second opportunity of seeing the wonderful engineering and grand scenery of the Boer Ghaut. The ascent of these mountains must in other days have been most laborious both for men and cattle. Descending into the plains felt like going into an oven, till the sea breeze cooled the air as we approached the coast.

Instead of stopping at Byculla, I proceeded to Boree

Bunda, the central station, which did not look worthy of so great a town, and took the tramway to Colaba, the point of Bombay which runs out into the sea, and thence back to Byculla, to see something of the city. It was unfortunate that during my stay in Bombay the weather was hazy, so that I did not get a good idea of the neighbourhood. The buildings around the esplanade are very fine, and the large open space by the sea is a great advantage to the town. Still it did not seem to me that Bombay could at all compare with Calcutta in the magnificence of its public buildings. Calcutta is a city of palaces. Bombay is the commercial capital of India, and at times has been wonderfully prosperous, though at others it has suffered from panic and great depression. Some persons advocate transferring the seat of the supreme Government here, but I apprehend no Viceroy is likely to accede to such an arrangement. Every Indian Government has a hill-station, and in this respect Bombay is worse off than any other. The Viceroy and his council spending the winter in Calcutta, the climate of which at that season is delightful, and the summer at Simla in sight of the snows of the Himalaya, may enjoy as good health as the British Cabinet, who are tied for great part of the year to London. They cannot be expected to wish for any change in their arrangements, and there seems no reason why such a change is desirable. For more than a century Calcutta has been the capital of British India, and in that country, where so much depends on maintaining a *régime* to which the natives are accustomed, it is peculiarly important to make no needless alterations. "Quieta non movere" is a good rule everywhere, especially in India. At Bombay I met Mr. Morton, with whom I had crossed in the "Alaska." He had travelled very leisurely, making a long stay at Hong-kong and Singapore, and had come here to commence his journey in India.

On the 26th I started with a Japanese gentleman to visit the caves of Elephanta, an island opposite Bombay. Taking a boat at Mazagon, we sailed for an hour and a half in the midst of islands, of which we could not see the outline clearly, on account of the haziness of the day, and amidst a fleet of boats with lateen sails, which looked very picturesque. After landing on the island, we ascended a long flight of stone steps till we reached the cave temple, which is cut out of the rock on the side of the hill. It is filled with figures of the Hindoo gods, among which a statue with three faces, Vishnu in the middle and Brahma and Seva on each side, is particularly remarkable. This old and curious temple is situated in the midst of palms and other tropical trees. There are other objects of interest higher up the hill, but the heat of the day made me afraid to attempt going farther.

In the evening I dined with the Governor at his residence at Pareil, meeting Captain Glyn, of the "Serapis," and Mr. Lee Warner, the secretary to Sir Philip Wodehouse. When I was at Calcutta, Captain Glyn was with the Prince in the North-West Provinces, but he returned afterwards to take the "Serapis" round to Bombay, where she was now waiting, having on board the menagerie which his Royal Highness collected in India.

The next day was Sunday, and in Byculla Church, near the hotel, I saw a tablet to Sir Robert Grant, author of some beautiful hymns, and ultimately Governor of Bombay. We had a very appropriate prayer read for the Prince's preservation during his Indian journey. I had not heard it before, and I was told afterwards that it was confined to the diocese of Bombay.

The tramway which runs from Byculla to Colaba is a great convenience. Tramways, like railways, must have a tendency to break down the system of caste. In the public conveyance the Brahmin finds himself sitting beside the Sudra, and he must either refuse to travel or submit to what his prejudices recoil at. The necessity of travelling forces him to humble his pride, and it is to be hoped that the result will tend to subvert the system. Still, the fall of an institution so engrained in the habits and feelings of the Hindoos must be slow, and we cannot expect any sudden change.

The 28th was my last day in India. I began by making some purchases of jewellery at the hotel. It is curious in India how the native shopkeepers frequent the hotels, offering their goods for sale. I called on Mr. Wood, late editor of the *Times of India*, and was much interested in conversing with a gentleman who views Indian affairs from a different standpoint from most of those whom I have met. The Indian official naturally looks with satisfaction on the existing order of things, while those who are outside the charmed circle of the covenanted service are disposed to criticize the proceedings of the Government. It is easy to find fault with every administration, and the rulers of the East are unquestionably open to animadversion on many points. Still, from the days of Clive to the present India has possessed a succession of statesmen who may compare with advantage with any similar succession in the history of the world, and it behoves those who blame to point out what course could have been more judicious than the one pursued.

I found among some of the younger civil servants dissatisfaction at the slow promotion of the service, dissatisfaction which has found a most able exponent at home in the person of Mr. Lowe. Mr. Lowe in speeches, first at the University of London, and afterwards in Parliament, called attention to the injustice inflicted on these gentlemen because the expectations held out to them by circulars issued by the Government had not been realized. I had the advantage of conversing on this subject with a member of the Indian Government who had been deputed to inquire into it, and who assured me that the complaint had been greatly exaggerated, and, in fact, had little foundation. All that the circular did was to point out that certain gentlemen entering the service had in a few years received certain salaries, but it is obvious that the expectations held out were subject to certain contingencies, and could not be considered as a guarantee on the part of the Government. In one or two years a greater number of appointments were given than were warranted by the requirements of the service, and consequently the successful competitors of the following years found their progress retarded by an excessive number of seniors. This was particularly the case in the north-west, where an undue number of civilians was sent, and some gentlemen, though not a large number in these provinces, had reason to complain of hardship. In other parts of India the complaint had little or no foundation. I cannot but regret that Mr. Lowe should have addressed the graduates of the University of London in a way that seemed to imply that he gave the sanction of his great reputation to the doctrine, that it was the vested interest of intellectual young Englishmen to govern the people of India. We ought to govern that great Empire with a view not to our own pecuniary profit, but to the prosperity and happiness of the vast population confided to our charge ; and the employment of natives in the highest positions is an object to be steadily borne in mind. In promoting this great object we should be deterred by no obstacles except those which have reference to the stability and security of the Empire. I much regretted to hear from Mr. Wood that the opposition between natives and Europeans seemed to him to be increasing. Perhaps the increasing number of Englishmen coming to India for purposes of commerce has conduced to this result.

Mr. Wood gave me the petition of the Sattara family

to the queen (formerly the chief family among the Mahrattas), praying for the restitution of that state. The annexation of Sattara was one of the first and most remarkable of the proceedings of Lord Dalhousie. It may be remembered that the deposition of a former Rajah led to long and interesting debates in the Court of Proprietors, where many of the most distinguished members of the Company, both directors and proprietors, protested against it. The influence of the Government of the day overruled the minority, which included Mr. Hume, so well known in the English political world, and Mr. Holt Mackenzie and Mr. Shepherd, so distinguished as Indian statesmen. The annexation was an unwise and unjust measure, the first of the series which led to the mutiny, and shook British power to its foundation. It has, however, passed into history, and belongs to that past it is impossible to recall.

The treatment of the native states is one of the many important questions which press on the Government. The annexation policy was abandoned after the mutiny, and the proclamation by which her Majesty assumed the control of India contains these words, "We hereby announce to the native princes of India, that all treaties and engagements made with them by or under the authority of the Honourable East India Company are by us accepted, and will be scrupulously maintained, and we look for the like observance on their part." This declaration is regarded as the Magna Charta of the native princes, and, on the whole, it has been scrupulously observed. Cases occasionally arise in which the causes of princes are decided by officials in a way which cannot be justified. The case of the deposed Nawab of Tonk may be cited, who, without discussing the question of his guilt or innocence, seems to me to have been tried and condemned by a secret tribunal worthy of the worst days of the Venetian Council of Ten. The remedy for such cases has been pointed out by two very high authorities, Sir Charles Wingfield and Sir Bartle Frere. It is "That the Sovereign should have at hand a tribunal forming a part of her Majesty's Privy Council, or possessing the same relation to the Crown, which may, at command, sit in judgment on questions of executive administration, whether appealed from, or referred by the Government of India, and which may decide such questions with an authority which shall be conclusive with Parliament and the public, as well as against any possible appellant." At present Parliament is the only Court of Appeal, and considering the great difficulties which any member of either House encounters in investigating such questions, that he is opposed by the Minister of the day, armed with all the information of the India Office, and that he has to plead the cause he undertakes in an assembly for the most part ignorant of and indifferent to Eastern affairs, it cannot be said to be satisfactory.

The close of Lord Northbrook's administration has been signalized by difficulties with two of the principal native princes. He pressed, in the strongest terms, that the young Nizam should meet the Prince of Wales at Bombay, and when Sir Salar Jung objected, on account of the state of his Sovereign's health, he threw doubt on the statement, and insisted on ascertaining the fact from a physician in whom he had confidence. This conduct is deeply to be lamented. It was uncourteous to so eminent a man as Sir Salar Jung, the most distinguished, by his talents, among the natives of India, to doubt his word, and it was dictatorial towards one of the principal Indian Courts. It may be said that all has passed over well, but mistakes of this kind do not develope their results at once. The injured native, for the moment, may suppress his feelings; but the indignity offered is not less keenly felt. The courtesy and consideration with which the Prince of Wales has treated the native princes has done much to smooth over present troubles; but as the recollection of his visit passes away, we may expect such mistakes to be remembered. Of some of them perhaps it may hereafter be said that the aggrieved party *μετόπισθεν ἔχει κότον ὄφρα τελέσσῃ*.

The Baroda case has attracted considerable attention in India, and has excited a certain amount of interest at home. The Guicowar (which, being interpreted, means the herdsman) of Baroda, has long been, and continues to be, one of the principal princes of India. Rank in India is regulated by the number of guns a great personage, whether British or native, is allowed for a salute, and the acquisition of an additional gun is an object of great ambition to a potentate. The Maharajah of Cashmere and the Guicowar rank at the head of the list. In 1870 Mulhar Rao succeeded to the throne of the Guicowars. Grave complaints of the misgovernment of the territory of Baroda were made to the Government of Bombay, who applied to the Government of India for authority to appoint a Commission of Bombay officers for the purpose of inquiring into and remedying it. On the 19th of September, 1873, the Viceroy replied that a Commission should be appointed; but that "it would most appropriately emanate from the Government of India." It would appear that in these important transactions injury to the public service may have arisen from the jealousy between the authorities of Calcutta and Bombay. The Calcutta officials assert that the power of the Bombay Government is too great for the advantageous working of the political system. On the other hand, the Bombay civilians complain that they are excluded from the great prizes of the Indian service. Be this as it may, Lord Northbrook assumed the conduct of Baroda affairs, and with him rests the responsibility of subsequent events.

A commission was appointed, which sat at Baroda, in November and December, 1875, and the result was that the Guicowar was allowed a year and a half to reform his administration. During this period an attempt was made to poison the British Resident, Colonel Phayre, and it was alleged that this attempt was made by the authority of the Guicowar. Colonel Phayre was a gentleman who had filled several important positions, though it is stated by the advocates of the

Guicowar that his appointment by the Bombay Government to Baroda was most improper, as he had been recently removed, for want of "skill and discretion," from another political situation in Scinde. There can be no question that the personal relations between the Guicowar and the Resident were most unsatisfactory. The Colonel believed, probably with great truth, that the misgovernment of Baroda was atrocious, and its Sovereign was surrounded with a set of men who were among the worst specimens of the courtiers who corrupt and ruin Eastern princes. On the other hand, Mulhar Rao had a personal antipathy to Colonel Phayre, whose exhortations to reform he resented. The intrigues of a native court are not to be fathomed. Whether the Guicowar was a party to the conspiracy to murder the Resident—whether, like Henry the Second in the case of Beckett, he simply expressed a wish that his enemy should be got rid of, or whether he was wholly innocent, are questions on which opinions will probably continue to differ. Those who have sat on juries in commercial cases know the difficulty of judging of conflicting testimony where both sides are anxious to speak the truth, while those who, whether as jurors or magistrates, have had to decide cases where witnesses are not to be believed on their oaths, have found this difficulty immeasurably increased. How arduous must, then, be the task of a tribunal which has to decide a cause where, from the inherent mendacity of the native witnesses, no reliance whatever can be placed on their testimony.

Two courses lay before Lord Northbrook, the Indian and the English. According to Indian precedent, he would have deputed a confidential commission to investigate the charge on the spot, and, having carefully considered the evidence produced before them, and the opinion they formed upon it, he would have pronounced his own decision. According to the system which we adopt in similar cases in England, he would have publicly tried the case by a competent tribunal, and would have been bound by their verdict. The Viceroy determined, in the first place, to pursue the latter course. He appointed a most eminent Commission publicly to investigate the charge. It consisted of Sir Richard Couch, Chief Justice of India, Sir Richard Meade, and Mr. Melville, on the part of the Government; and of Scindiah, the Maharajah of Jeypore, and Sir Dinkah Rao, on the part of the natives. More eminent men can hardly be found in India, and it was supposed the Government of India was acting with the impartiality of that of England. It was true that Holkar, fearing lest the tribunal should not be confided in, refused to be a member, but for the time it was thought that the decision was really in the hands of the Commissioners. They met and investigated the charge at great length. The public nature of the inquiry enabled the Guicowar to retain the services of one of the most eminent members of the English bar, and the eloquence of Serjeant Ballantine did much to create throughout the whole population of India a feeling in favour of their fellow-countryman. After a prolonged investigation the Commissioners differed, the three Englishmen pronouncing the Guicowar guilty, the three natives acquitting him. According to every English idea the prince was acquitted. When an Englishman has been tried, and a verdict of Guilty has not been returned, nothing is more obvious than that no further proceedings should be taken. Among the judges acquitting were two of the ablest and most powerful Indian princes, and it was not only courtesy but policy to respect their verdict.

It is evident that Lord Northbrook, when he appointed the Commission, had felt sure of a conviction, of which he was deprived by the eloquence of Serjeant Ballantine; foiled in this expectation, he fell back on the charge of misgovernment. After the report of the first Commission he had allowed Mulhar Rao to the close of 1875 to reform the abuses of his State. Under the disappointment of the failure of the trial, he disregarded the arrangement he had himself entered into, deposed the Guicowar for maladministration, expelled him from his kingdom, and placed a relative on the vacant throne. It is right to add, that he succeeded in placing the Government under one of the most distinguished native statesmen, Sir Madova Rao, under whose enlightened administration we may hope that the necessary reforms may be effected.

The Baroda episode in Lord Northbrook's administration is one to be deeply regretted. Granting that the misgovernment was of the most atrocious description, admitting that the deposed Guicowar was the most vicious of Eastern potentates, assuming that his complicity in the conspiracy to poison Colonel Phayre was proved beyond all cavil, making every allowance which can be asked for on the part of the Government, the whole course of proceeding can only be regarded as most unfortunate. To disregard an acquittal, and to anticipate a period granted for reformation, seems conduct more worthy of a low-class attorney than an eminent statesman, while its effects on the minds of the people of India must be to shake their confidence in British justice. It cannot but be prejudicial to the respect with which we wish them to regard the Government, that they should see the verdict of their most honoured and respected representatives slighted, and the scion of one of their noblest houses first tried and acquitted, then condemned and punished. To the high-handed exercise of power they were accustomed under former rulers, but this mockery of justice is new in India.

It was rather less than eight weeks since I had landed at Madras, and it is wonderful to consider how much can be done by the aid of railways in that short time. Without travelling particularly fast, I had visited places which thirty years ago many of the oldest Indians had never seen. Owing to the improved means of communication, the leading towns of British India are for the most part easily accessible, though as yet the capitals of the native princes are more difficult to reach. Of course a journey in India, even were it much longer and more extended than mine, can only enable the traveller to give a cursory glance at that wonderful country. There is much which time does not permit to be seen. I particularly regretted that I had not the opportunity of coming in contact with those holy and devoted men who are labouring as missionaries in India. It seems to me that there can be no question that the wonderful power which God has given to England in India is designed to promote the spread of Christianity among the vast populations of the Peninsula, and that while there is a call to preach the Gospel in every country, that call is particularly loud from our own dependencies, and particularly from India.

No one can travel in India without feeling an increased interest in the country and its people. We are too apt to forget how closely the prosperity of England and the very existence of British power are linked with the possession of India. Without India and the Colonies Great Britain would sink to the position of Holland—a country important from its commerce, but of secondary weight in the councils of the world. Hence everything which concerns its welfare should be matter of the deepest interest. We can but heartily desire that the vast population under British sway may increase in material prosperity, may develope in moral greatness, and, above all, by God's blessing, may receive that holy religion which breathes nothing but peace on earth and good-will to the children of men.

In the afternoon I went down to the P. and O. wharf at Mazagon, whence a tender took the passengers on board the "Peshawur," Captain White. About half-past seven the mail came on board, and we commenced our voyage. As long as I remained on deck the flashing light on Colaba Point continued to be visible. Thus I took leave of India,—

> "It may be for years, or it may be for ever."

The six following days were passed at sea, averaging a run of 273 miles a day. The distance from Bombay to Aden is about 1650 miles. The "Peshawur," though not very fast, is a fine ship of nearly 4000 tons. We had nearly 100 passengers, which made the ship rather full, especially at meals. Fortunately for me, neither of the two gentlemen who had been put down to share my cabin turned up, so I had a state-room to myself. The company included several Australians, who, instead of taking the direct boat at Galle, had come on to Bombay and waited for our steamer. There were also two reporters, who had been following the Prince through his Indian tour. The principal Indians on board were Mr. Eden, whom I had met in Calcutta, and Mr. Scoble, the Advocate-General of Bombay. There were also several officers, who were only going to Aden. I was surprised to hear from them that the frontier force, consisting of 12,000 men, is under the Governor of the Punjaub, and not under the Commander-in-Chief, though the troops at Peshawur are under the latter. This seems an odd arrangement, but the reason given is that the frontier soldiers have police duties to discharge.

On Sunday, March 5th, the Rev. Mr. Steed, a chaplain from Poona, performed service. In the afternoon we had a sad sight. A poor woman in the second class had died in the night, and owing to the heat we could not take the body to Aden. It was the first time I had witnessed the striking and solemn spectacle of seeing the remains of a fellow-creature committed to the deep. The service was read, and the coffin at the proper moment thrown into the sea.

About five the land by Aden came into sight, and at 10.20 p.m. we dropped anchor. I went with a party on shore to the hotel, where many of my companions bought ostrich feathers, which seemed the great article of trade. The town looked well by moonlight, and the southern cross, though to some extent obscured by the moon, was fine. Aden is situated in latitude 12° 45′, and must be intensely hot. The administration is under the Government of Bombay. A regiment is kept here, and the 55th, some of whose officers had been on board the "Peshawur," had just arrived. It must be a most unpleasant station, as the heat is great and the town is surrounded by desert. I was told a curious thing about the telegraph. Every message comes here to be transmitted to India, but the clerk is not allowed to divulge the news, as the community have refused the payment demanded by the company. The consequence is, that the inhabitants of Aden have to wait the arrival of the steamer from Bombay to learn news which has passed through more than a week before.

We weighed anchor about four in the morning of the 6th, and steered west for the Straits of Bab-el-Mandeb, which we passed at mid-day and entered the Red Sea. We passed Perim, where an unfortunate garrison is kept to guard the entrance to the sea. A good story is told of an officer who solicited an extension of his time of service here. The authorities readily granted so unusual a request, and it was not till some time afterwards that it was discovered that, instead of remaining in exile on a desert island, the young gentleman had put himself on board the P. and O., visited London, and returned ere his term of duty was ended. The distance from Aden to Suez is more than 1300 miles, which we accomplished in five days. The boat was advertised to be at Aden on Tuesday, and at Suez on the following Monday, so that we saved two days. The voyage up the Red Sea was very pleasant—a great contrast to what many travellers experience, especially when going south. In the summer months the heat appears to be almost insupportable, and deaths are often occasioned by it. On the 9th we crossed the tropic, and on the 10th saw Ras Mahomet, the high promontory between the gulfs of Akaba and Suez. We sailed up the Gulf of Suez, having on our right the chain of Sinai, where the law was given to Moses.

At 5 a.m. on Saturday, the 11th, we reached Suez, where the steamer divides her passengers, those going through the canal to Gibraltar and Southampton remaining on board, while those who are bound for Italy land. By the latter route you have the choice of proceeding either to Brindisi, Ancona, or Venice. I had at first contemplated Venice, but impatience to get home ultimately induced me to stop at Brindisi. The steamer proceeded through the canal, which was, I understood, likely to be rather a slow process. Throughout the East I heard much discussion about the canal, and the Government purchase of shares was generally approved. Whatever may be thought about the general question of Turkey, there can be no doubt of the vital importance to England of keeping the road to India through Egypt open. Were Egypt in the hands of a hostile power, the very existence of the British empire would be in danger.

Landing at the mouth of the canal, we proceeded by train to the town of Suez, where we spent the day at the hotel. I walked about the town with Colonel Barrow, the Commander of the Oude constabulary, with whom I travelled as far as Paris. We were struck with the contrast with India. Here the streets are narrow and the bazaars covered. There the streets are wide, and, in spite of the great heat, you do not see covered bazaars. Much of the town is in ruins, and, in spite of the number of Europeans residing in it, it presents a thoroughly Oriental appearance. The donkey-boys are very amusing. On emerging from the hotel I was greeted with the exhortations, "Take Sir Roger Tichborne, the Claimant, very good donkey!" "Take Dr. Kenealy, good donkey!" On arriving at home I asked my brother-in-law, who sits on the same bench with him in the House, to tell the worthy Doctor that his fame had extended to Suez.

At half-past six the train left Suez for Alexandria. It struck me that it would be worth the attention of the Postmaster-General whether the transit through Egypt could not be expedited. When Captain White found he could not save Friday's train, he reduced his speed, and we had twelve hours' detention at Suez and six at Alexandria. In our case nearly twenty-four hours might have been saved in the transit of the mail, as we afterwards lost six more at Bologna. Being before our time, this probably was not regarded.

The journey through Egypt was accomplished at a fair speed. In the earlier part of the ride, where the line is near the canal, it was too dark to see anything, but the rising of the moon showed us something of the different channels of the Nile, which we crossed. About 6 a.m. we reached Alexandria, and went on board the "Kashgar," Captain Baker. I had not been in Alexandria for twenty-six years, but as it was Sunday morning I did not like to be sight-seeing. I therefore contented myself with viewing the imposing city and Pompey's Pillar from the sea, as well as Pharos, within which our ship was lying. At noon we started, and about two lost sight of Pharos, the last object which remained visible.

The "Kashgar" is a very fast ship, and easily accomplished the run of 825 miles in seventy-two hours. In the afternoon of the 13th we saw the snowy heights of Mount Ida, in Crete, and continued till midnight near the country of Minos and Idomeneus. On the morning of the 14th we were in sight of Cape Matapan, and passed the Bay of Navarino, so memorable both in ancient and modern history, which reminded me that a year before I had been in a steamer which was driven into it by stress of weather. In the afternoon we passed Zante, "il fiore di Levante," and saw Cephalonia, and Ithaca, the island of Ulysses, in the distance.

On going on deck on the morning of the 15th I found we were approaching Otranto, and at half-past twelve we arrived at Brindisi.

"Brundisium longæ finis chartæque viæque."

It was not, of course, the termination of my wanderings, but it is the last place in regard to which I need trespass on the attention of the indulgent reader who has followed me thus far. Suffice it to say that leaving immediately with the mail, and taking the well-known route through Italy and France (then rendered remarkable by great inundations of the Soane and the Seine) I found myself at half-past six in the morning of Saturday, the 18th of March, in the City of London, having, through the protecting care of a merciful Providence, travelled 34,000 miles without illness or accident of any kind.

INDEX.